ASHE Higher Education Report: Volume 33, Number 4
Kelly Ward, Lisa E. Wolf-Wendel, Series Editors

Reinventing Undergraduate Education: Engaging College Students in Research and Creative Activities

Shouping Hu
Kathyrine Scheuch
Robert Schwartz
Joy Gaston Gayles
Shaoqing Li

Reinventing Undergraduate Education: Engaging College Students in Research and Creative Activities
Shouping Hu, Kathyrine Scheuch, Robert Schwartz,
Joy Gaston Gayles, and Shaoqing Li
ASHE Higher Education Report: Volume 33, Number 4
Kelly Ward, Lisa E. Wolf-Wendel, Series Editors

ISSN 1551-6970   electronic ISSN 1554-6306   ISBN 978-0-4702-8358-5

The ASHE Higher Education Report is part of the Jossey-Bass Higher and Adult Education Series and is published six times a year by Wiley Subscription Services, Inc., A Wiley Company, at Jossey-Bass, 989 Market Street, San Francisco, California 94103-1741.

For subscription information, see the Back Issue/Subscription Order Form in the back of this volume.

CALL FOR PROPOSALS: Prospective authors are strongly encouraged to contact Kelly Ward (kaward@wsu.edu) or Lisa Wolf-Wendel (lwolf@ku.edu). See "About the ASHE Higher Education Report Series" in the back of this volume.

Visit the Jossey-Bass Web site at **www.josseybass.com.**

Printed in the United States of America on acid-free recycled paper.

The ASHE Higher Education Report is indexed in CIJE: Current Index to Journals in Education (ERIC), Current Abstracts (EBSCO), Education Index/Abstracts (H.W. Wilson), ERIC Database (Education Resources Information Center), Higher Education Abstracts (Claremont Graduate University), IBR & IBZ: International Bibliographies of Periodical Literature (K.G. Saur), and Resources in Education (ERIC).

Advisory Board

The ASHE Higher Education Report Series is sponsored by the Association for the Study of Higher Education (ASHE), which provides an editorial advisory board of ASHE members.

Contents

Executive Summary

Concerns about the quality of undergraduate education have prompted increasing calls for improved quality of the baccalaureate experience and student learning from colleges and universities (Association of American Colleges and Universities, 2002a; Bok, 2006; Education Commission of the States, 1995; Kellogg Commission on the Future of State and Land-Grant Universities, 1997; National Commission on the Future of Higher Education, 2006; Wingspread Group on Higher Education, 1993). One of the approaches to reform is to engage undergraduate students in research and creative activities (Association of American Colleges and Universities, 2007; Boyer Commission on Educating Undergraduates in the Research University, 1998; Council on Undergraduate Research and National Conference for Undergraduate Research, 2005; Karukstis and Elgren, 2007).

This innovative strategy has gained some steam after the initial release of the Boyer Commission report in 1998 (Boyer Commission on Educating Undergraduates in the Research University, 2003; Hu, Kuh, and Gayles, 2007; Karukstis and Elgren, 2007; Katkin, 2003). To sustain this momentum, however, it is necessary to understand how engagement in research and creative activities could affect student outcomes from college, what factors are related to student engagement, and what effective policies and practices can be adopted and implemented by colleges and universities to promote undergraduate engagement in those activities. This report systematically synthesizes existing literature and reviews policies and practices to provide evidence-based answers to these questions (Slavin, 2002).

What Are Undergraduate Research and Creative Activities?

Undergraduate research can be defined as "an inquiry or investigation conducted by an undergraduate that makes an original intellectual or creative contribution to the discipline" (Council on Undergraduate Research, 2003). The types of undergraduate research and creative activities vary, both across and in disciplines. For example, activities in the traditional science, technology, engineering, and mathematics fields can be experiments in laboratory environments, contrasted to activities such as performing arts or archival analysis in the humanities. The objectives of undergraduate research and creative activities can also vary. Some argue the importance of original contribution to the literature as a goal, while others emphasize the educational and socializing functions of such activities on students.

What Conceptual Evidence Exists of the Effectiveness on Student Outcomes of Engagement in Research and Creative Activities?

Engaging undergraduates in research and creative activities reflects principles of the constructivist learning theories and several well-known educational practices. Mentoring by and interaction with faculty advisors or others in research and creative projects could serve as a "scaffold" in enhancing student learning. Research and creative activities also reflect the features of experiential learning, problem-based learning, and inquiry-based learning—models conducive to student learning and development. Moreover, participation in research and creative activities helps immerse students in an environment with heightened academic and social interactions with faculty, graduate students, and peers and further socializes students into the academic and social systems of the institution and the profession.

What Empirical Evidence Exists of the Effects of Engagement in Research and Creative Activities on Student Outcomes?

Students' engagement in research and creative activities during the college years is associated with a variety of outcomes in both the cognitive and affective domains (Astin, 1993a, 1993b; Bloom, 1956; Krathwohl, Bloom, and Bertram, 1973). It positively affects students' academic performance, critical thinking, satisfaction, persistence, choice of major and career, and other desirable outcomes. The effects are even more evident for certain outcomes regarding special student populations such as racial and ethnic minorities. Consistent with the evidence from Pascarella and Terenzini's synthesis (2005), engaging students in undergraduate research and creative activities is "relatively potent" in producing some desirable outcomes (p. 406).

What Factors Are Associated with Students' Engagement in Research and Creative Activities?

Analyses of data from the National Survey of Student Engagement and the College Student Experience Questionnaire indicate the different overall patterns of engagement in research and creative activities by students of different backgrounds, in different colleges, and in different disciplines. Foreign students, students in biological and physical sciences, and students in baccalaureate and liberal arts colleges appear to participate in research activities at higher rates. Existing literature reports the net effects of those factors but also points to the importance of institutional conditions in promoting students' engagement in research and creative activities.

How Can Colleges and Universities Promote Students' Engagement in Research and Creative Activities?

To promote undergraduate participation in research and creative activities in college, it is necessary to enhance the understanding of the effects of such activities in student learning and personal development among faculty, students, staff members, and administrators. Colleges and universities can purposefully integrate inquiry-oriented activities in the curriculum, institutionalize research-supportive programs, and foster a campus culture that values inquiry-based undergraduate education to promote students' engagement in research and creative activities (Karukstis and Elgren, 2007).

Undergraduate research and creative activities show great promise in promoting student learning and personal development. As accountability toward student learning in higher education intensifies, efforts in engaging undergraduates in research and creative activities can help renew institutional commitments to educating students and helping students succeed in college.

Foreword

External constituencies (accrediting agencies, students, parents, legislators and policy makers) are attempting to hold colleges and universities accountable for student learning outcomes. Colleges and universities, in response, are throwing resources at the issue—trying to figure out a way to prove (or at least demonstrate) that they are having a positive effect on student learning. One means of proving a positive outcome is to engage in practices that we know to be effective. Engaging undergraduates in research and creative activities outside of the classroom is one such effective practice.

This is an important monograph because it explores the ins and outs of one of the most important and effective educational practices available to undergraduates—extracurricular research. This monograph is a great companion piece to the ASHE monograph by Kuh and his colleagues (2007) on how to facilitate student success, as it offers an in-depth exploration of a particular means to create an engaging educational environment and the effects of such an endeavor on undergraduates.

Engaging students in research and creative experiences represents a high-impact activity that is the epitome of accepted best practices in undergraduate education. Like service learning, learning communities, and study abroad, undergraduate research embodies all of the characteristics outlined by Chickering and Gamson (1991) in their following list of best practices for undergraduate education.

- Encourages student faculty contact.
- Encourages cooperation among students
- Encourages active learning

- Gives prompt feedback
- Emphasizes time on task
- Communicates high expectations
- Respects diverse talents and ways of learning

Undergraduate research is truly one of the very few extracurricular activities that boasts such an impressive overlap with undergraduate best practices. Unfortunately, many college students are never given the opportunity to engage in these kinds of activities. Undergraduate research doesn't just happen—it needs coordination, support, and attention. It is one of those institutional activities that require collaboration across units and between student affairs and academic affairs. Faculty need incentives and recognition for engaging in these practices and students need to know the array of opportunities available. These connections can happen on an ad hoc basis but in order to increase the opportunities undergraduate research needs to be supported institutionally.

Colleges and universities still need to be convinced that these activities warrant increased attention and resources. This monograph provides faculty, administrators, student affairs staff, and researchers excellent information about the benefits and intricacies of creating a strong undergraduate research program. The chapter providing examples of how different types of colleges and different disciplines have created these opportunities is especially useful to the field.

Lisa E. Wolf-Wendel
Series Editor

Acknowledgments

This monograph is the outcome of an intellectual collaboration. Each team member brought a different perspective and made scholarly contributions, with a common interest in promoting student learning in higher education. We are indebted to many scholars and practitioners whose work has opened the opportunity for us to write this monograph. In particular, we would like to thank George Kuh for his intellectual leadership in studying college student engagement and his scholarly influence on many of us. George also kindly allowed us to use recent data from the National Survey of Student Engagement for this project. Comments and suggestions from the anonymous reviewers and the series editor Lisa Wolf-Wendel were extremely helpful in improving the quality of the final product. Lisa's insights into theories of student engagement, involvement, and integration have helped refine our thinking about the relevance of those theories to undergraduate research and creative activities. Finally, Shaoqing and Shouping would like to thank their lovely boys Aaron and Alex for the joy and happiness they bring into their lives.

 Published online in Wiley InterScience
(www.interscience.wiley.com) • DOI: 10.1002/aehe.3304

Learning Imperatives in Undergraduate Education

UNDERGRADUATE EDUCATION has been under constant scrutiny for decades in the United States. The persistent discontent with higher education is evident from books such as *Our Underachieving Colleges* (Bok, 2006) as well as from numerous reports by various groups inside and outside the academy, including the Association of American Colleges and Universities (2002a), the Boyer Commission on Educating Undergraduates in the Research University (1998), the National Commission on the Future of Higher Education (2006), and the Wingspread Group on Higher Education (1993). A salient and recurring concern is the quality of undergraduate education. According to the Wingspread Group on Higher Education, "a disturbing and dangerous mismatch exists between what American society needs of higher education and what it is receiving. Nowhere is the mismatch more dangerous than in the quality of undergraduate preparation" (1993, p. 1). Several prominent commissions shared this sentiment. For instance, the Boyer Commission on Educating Undergraduates in the Research University stated forcefully in its 1998 report that "many students graduate having accumulated whatever number of courses is required, but still lacking a coherent body of knowledge or any inkling as to how one sort of information might relate to others. And all too often they graduate without knowing how to think logically, write clearly, or speak coherently" (p. 6). The National Commission on the Future of Higher Education (2006) was "disturbed by evidence that the quality of student learning at U.S. colleges and universities is inadequate and, in some cases, declining" (p. 3). It suggested that "these shortcomings have real-world consequences. Employers report repeatedly that many new graduates they hire are not prepared to work, lacking the critical thinking, writing and problem-solving skills needed in today's workplaces. In addition, business and government leaders have repeatedly and urgently called for workers at all stages of life to continually upgrade their academic and practical skills" (p. 3).

Promoting student learning from higher education has become a national imperative that drives recent calls for the reform of higher education. Various proposals have been circulated on the strategies that colleges and universities can use to improve the quality of undergraduate education. One such proposal is to engage undergraduate students in research and creative activities. For example, the Boyer Commission on Educating Undergraduates in the Research University (1998) proposed that higher education institutions engage undergraduate students in knowledge discovery by creating an inquiry-based learning experience for students. In 2005, the Council on Undergraduate Research (CUR) and the National Conference for Undergraduate Research (NCUR) issued a joint statement in support of the Boyer Commission's recommendation of engaging undergraduate students in research and creative activities. These two organizations stated that undergraduate research is "a comprehensive curricular innovation and major reform in contemporary American undergraduate education and scholarship" and "the pedagogy for the twenty-first century."

A good number of universities have taken this recommendation seriously by redirecting resources and campus energies toward engaging undergraduate students in research and creative activities (Association of American Colleges and Universities, 2007; Boyer Commission on Educating Undergraduates in the Research University, 2003; Hu, Kuh, and Gayles, 2007; Karukstis and Elgren, 2007). A systematic understanding of the causes and effects of undergraduate student engagement in research and creative activities is still lacking, however (Karukstis and Elgren, 2007). To improve the quality of undergraduate education, it is necessary to understand what the effects are for undergraduate students who engage in research and creative activities and what factors may promote or hinder student engagement in such activities.

Facing another round of fiscal crises, higher education institutions will have to be more strategic in using their limited financial resources on various programs and initiatives. This issue is even more critical as "accountability" becomes a buzzword in the policy arena at all levels (Hu, 2005; National

Commission on the Future of Higher Education, 2006). A systematic and comprehensive synthesis like this study could help reveal what works in improving student learning and aid financial decisions in higher education.

The purpose of this monograph is to present both the empirical and conceptual evidence of the causes and effects of undergraduate student engagement in research and creative activities (Krathwohl, 1998). Four questions guide this report:

1. What are the intellectual underpinnings of engaging undergraduate students in research and creative activities?
2. What are the effects of engaging in research and creative activities on a variety of outcomes for undergraduate students?
3. What are the correlates of students' engagement in research and creative activities? Are there discernible differences in the patterns of engagement for students of different backgrounds, those enrolled in different types of institutions, or in colleges at different historical times?
4. What initiatives, both common and distinctive, have colleges and universities made in engaging undergraduate students in research and creative activities?

This monograph first describes the scope of undergraduate research and creative activities, the variations of such activities across and within disciplines, and their historical evolution. Second, it discusses constructivist learning theories and exemplary educational practices to distill conceptual support for engaging in undergraduate research and creative activities. Empirical studies are then reviewed to demonstrate the effects of such activities on student outcomes. Subsequently, the report identifies the factors that are related to student engagement in research activities and presents the patterns of student engagement with respect to student and institutional characteristics, disciplinary differences, and longitudinal trends. Finally, the report documents institutional efforts in engaging students in research activities and analyzes program features that are conducive to student engagement.

Given the increasing discontent with the quality of undergraduate education, this report is intended for a broad base of readership, ranging from academic researchers, higher education administrators, and leaders in various professional organizations. We anticipate it will be of interest to university presidents, provosts, and deans who are responsible for undergraduate studies, academic deans and department chairs, and faculty members who are working with undergraduate students on various projects. It should also be of interest to the leadership in various groups and organizations interested in improving the quality of undergraduate education such as the National Science Foundation (NSF), the CUR, the NCUR, and the American Association of Colleges and Universities (AAC&U). Finally, given the attention to undergraduate research experiences for students of different backgrounds and the potential influences of those experiences on students' educational and career choices, this report may prove valuable for public policymakers who are concerned about equal educational opportunity and human resource development in critical areas such as science, technology, engineering, and mathematics.

Description of Undergraduate Research and Creative Activities

UNDERGRADUATE RESEARCH AND CREATIVE ACTIVITIES exist in a wide range of forms in different disciplines in colleges and universities. This section discusses the different perspectives on undergraduate research and creative activities, points out variations of such activities among disciplines, and briefly describes the historical evolution that leads to the emergence of undergraduate research and creative activities in American higher education.

Defining Undergraduate Research and Creative Activities

The difficulty in defining undergraduate research and creative activities is complicated in part by the conception of the objectives of undergraduate research (Association of American Colleges and Universities, 2007; Brubacher, 1982; Geiger, 2004; Kinkead, 2003; Lucas, 1996). Undergraduate research and creative activities reflect the idea of advancing the knowledge frontier. Although producing original results could be the goal for some educators, learning the research process or cultivating the cognitive and mechanical skills necessary to execute a study could be the goal for others (Kremer and Bringle, 1990; Seago, 1992; Siebert, 1988). Some even consider undergraduate research activities a means of initiating interest in research careers and fostering an appreciation for the research process in students (Seymour, Hunter, Laursen, and Deantoni, 2004; Thompson, McNeil, Sherwood, and Stark, 2001). Recently,

Elgren and Hensel (2006) provided a comprehensive perspective on the objectives of undergraduate research and creative activities: promoting student learning outcomes, helping develop a faculty mentor's scholarly agenda, and contributing to the field. Therefore, undergraduate research and creative activities should intend to benefit participating students, faculty mentors, and the field as a whole.

Given the wide range of perspectives, we adopt the inclusive definition of undergraduate research offered by the Council on Undergraduate Research. The CUR defines undergraduate research as "an inquiry or investigation conducted by an undergraduate that makes an original intellectual or creative contribution to the discipline" (2003). The types of activities range from work in laboratories to music composition, works of art, field experiments, and document analysis (Kinkead, 2003; Strassburger, 1995).

Undergraduate research activities have similar characteristics, regardless of discipline. Whether the activity involves writing a play, composing a musical score, or replicating genes, students are challenged to be resourceful in their thinking to produce an artistic product, critically evaluate existing knowledge, or identify and solve problems in their particular disciplines. Additionally, the quality of work generated by undergraduate researchers sometimes yields concrete outcomes such as publication in peer-reviewed journals or acceptance of research abstracts for presentation of a paper or poster at professional conferences; such activities introduce and socialize students to experts in their fields (Kinkead, 2003; Russell, 2006; Seymour, Hunter, Laursen, and Deantoni, 2004). Undergraduate research and scholarly and creative activities typically involve the following characteristics (Kinkead, 2003; Kremer and Bringle, 1990; Lanza, 1988; Lanza and Smith, 1988; Russell, 2006; Seymour, Hunter, Laursen, and Deantoni, 2004):

A faculty mentor who guides and supervises the undergraduate student;

Formulation of a project (independent or part of a faculty member's ongoing work);

Preparation of a research proposal describing research that will be carried out;

An introduction to and training in research methodologies, scholarly inquiry, or creative processes of a discipline;

Data collection or background research;

Analysis of the data;

A written or oral report of results (perhaps for publication or presentation);

Presentation of results at a symposium, conference, festival, or professional meeting

Hakim (1998) suggested that undergraduate research has four basic characteristics: mentorship, originality, acceptability, and dissemination. Mentorship involves substantial interaction between faculty and students. Hakim indicated that the focus of the mentor relationship is on student outcomes as opposed to the outcomes of research and teaching. Originality assumes that the student takes an active part in the creation of new knowledge through active participation in the research project. It is most likely to happen when the project poses a new question or hypothesis or a twist on an old question, as opposed to replicating a previous study.

Another characteristic of undergraduate research is that the student learns the acceptable methods of inquiry related to his or her field of study. A research project should conclude with the production, dissemination, and critique of a final product. This product could be in the form of a research paper presented at a conference or symposium, a poster session at a conference, or a manuscript submitted for publication in an academic journal.

Graff (2006) offered another way of understanding undergraduate research that institutions and disciplines can adopt regardless of differences in programmatic structure. He suggested that a key characteristic distinguishing undergraduate research from other intellectual activities is the notion of "entering the current conversation of a particular field in a significant way." It is a simple but important concept for undergraduates to understand because most see research as collecting data and ideas that stops short of using the data to enter the conversation in a field of study. In other words, a key component of undergraduate research should include the process of framing the results of a study in response to a current discussion in the field as opposed to simply presenting the findings of a study in a vacuum outside this context. A more meaningful process for students is to discuss their findings in light of what others have written on the topic.

Although these elements vary depending on the type of work that is being carried out, the premise is the same: students cultivate the necessary skills to design and execute a project in the same manner as academics or professionals in their fields perform research or creative work. These active learning activities help improve students' educational experiences while allowing more in-depth exploration of their disciplines.

The intended outcomes for undergraduate student engagement in research and creative activities generally fall in common categories (Kremer and Bringle, 1990; Peppas, 1981; Thompson, McNeil, Sherwood, and Stark, 2001; Wray, 2000; McKinney, Saxe, and Cobb, 1998):

Enhance undergraduate education through hands-on learning activities that cultivate students' analytical, logical, and creative thinking, problem solving, curiosity, written and oral skills, and self-reliance;

Provide concrete examples of how theories and principles are applied to find solutions to problems;

Introduce students to the methods of inquiry in their disciplines and foster appreciation of the research process;

Stimulate students' interest in pursuing academic or research careers;

Help socialize students to their respective professions and academic fields;

Prepare students for advanced graduate or professional education;

Sufficiently train students to compete in an increasingly global market as future leaders, especially for the United States.

Disciplinary Differences in Undergraduate Research and Creative Activities

Providing hands-on experiences for undergraduates is certainly more straightforward in some disciplines than in others. Ishiyama (2002) points out that many disciplines in social sciences and humanities (with the exception of psychology) do not use the experimental method in their research. Research that uses the experimental method can more readily incorporate undergraduates in carrying out a portion of the study. In the humanities and social sciences, however, scholarly work is performed in a more exhaustive and in-depth field research of social, political, and cultural phenomena that do not always lend themselves to quantification (Ishiyama, 2002).

For science, technology, engineering, and mathematics (STEM), however, students can assume progressive roles in the laboratory and contribute to an overall experiment. A student can enter a project without specific work experience and receive technical training that can lead to more complex tasks. Kremer and Bringle (1990) outlined three types of undergraduate research activities:

1. *Teaching model:* a common strategy used to teach students how research has been conducted, to impart some research skills, and to provide a few opportunities to use these skills;
2. *Technician model:* the undergraduate takes only low-skilled roles; and
3. *Colleague model:* students take a significant role in many phases of the research.

These three models provide a general description of the activities students are involved in with undergraduate research in a scientific setting. Kremer and Bringle (1990) describe the teaching function of undergraduate research as a process of learning how to do research by conducting canned experiments. These types of projects provide the student with the problem, hypothesis, description of procedures, list of materials, and method of data analysis (Kremer and Bringle, 1990). Prepackaged experiments, however, provide limited insight into an authentic research experience because such processes involve replicating predetermined results (Powell and Stiller, 2005). On the other hand, students who are involved in ongoing research fill two qualitatively different roles: technician or colleague.

In ongoing research, students serving as technicians perform basic tasks as laboratory assistants and may code data or prepare glassware. Kremer and Bringle (1990) point out that "faculty who use this model believe that students are not sufficiently skilled or trained to contribute in more substantive ways" (p. 1). Such work provides menial technical training for students and may instill the importance of accuracy in data coding, for example, but the educative value of such tasks to the goal of learning about inquiry is uncertain. The colleague model provides a more sophisticated method of involving students in ongoing research. Students who serve as colleagues on a research project work in collaboration with the professor or researcher to develop the hypothesis, research design, and experimental procedure (Kremer and Bringle, 1990). Students as colleagues are involved in open-ended questions and are sometimes required to learn new skills to carry out certain aspects of the research. The contrast in experiences between the technician and colleague models is a prime example of how undergraduate research experiences involve diverse levels of complexity. Similarly, the value added to a student's educational experience varies accordingly.

Undergraduate engagement in research can take a different form in the humanities and social sciences. Current discussions about undergraduate research and creative activities focus on what opportunities can be provided in the humanities and social sciences, as the nature of some research activities precludes collaboration with students or requires higher-order skills to carry out work as it is accomplished in the field. Some faculty members may not feel undergraduates possess the required skill levels to carry out scholarly work in these areas (Ishiyama, 2002; Kinkead, 2003). As a result, undergraduates are not as easily incorporated in work with their professors as they are in the STEM fields.

In the humanities, for example, based on one's scholarly knowledge of an area, research is carried out in a solitary manner whereby the researcher may critically review materials to answer a research question. Many times, these disciplines require skills beyond what is provided in the undergraduate curriculum for in-depth understanding and analysis of a question. McDorman (2004) cites the personal, solitary, and individual nature of humanities research and the more advanced theoretical elements of the discipline that are "generally challenging for students to productively grasp in a short period of time" (p. 39) as barriers to including undergraduates in research projects. Further, some academics in these fields question the validity of work carried out by undergraduates (because, for example, research is defined as original work) or the value that such activities contribute to undergraduates' education (Werner and Sorum, 2003). Scholars in these fields are reluctant to collaborate with undergraduates because it is not a disciplinary norm, while others view such work as detrimental to their own scholarly development (Werner and Sorum, 2003; McDorman, 2004).

This is not to say, however, that undergraduates cannot be incorporated in active learning experiences in these disciplines. On the contrary, some faculty members have formulated ways of introducing students to inquiry methods. Based on his experience working with students on projects, McDorman (2004) identified three collaborative approaches to undergraduate research in the humanities: faculty-driven collaboration, faculty modeling, and student-driven collaboration.

For the faculty-driven model, the professor takes primary responsibility for designing and leading the project while students take an active role in contributing to the final product. In his example, McDorman describes how he guided three students through an independent study project that he created with the goal of producing a coauthored essay to be submitted to a journal. Throughout the semester, the group read about film criticism, composed a written analysis of the films under review, and met frequently for critical discussions. Together, they produced an article that was thoroughly edited by the faculty member and submitted for publication.

Under the faculty modeling method, McDorman designed and structured his class as a workshop during which students reviewed each other's work (as well as the professor's) and provided feedback to each other. This model, according to the author, prompted students to put more effort into their papers because their peers were reviewing their work; it also allowed them to see that their professor encountered some of the same vagaries of research that they experienced. All the workshop participants presented their work in class and submitted a final essay at the end of the semester.

The student-driven collaboration model places the responsibility of moving the work forward on the student. The professor provides guidance in the form of suggested readings or feedback on the student's draft. McDorman acknowledged that the process was slow at times as the student wrestled with further refining the work, but this step was necessary for the student to learn about academic writing for publication.

Both Rogers (2003) and McDorman (2004) extended their faculty modeling workshops to another level for students who wanted to continue their research experiences. McDorman used student-driven collaboration to introduce his student to advanced academic writing that ultimately resulted in publication of a coauthored article. Rogers's workshop, on the other hand, provided his students with the skills necessary to perform archival research with him in Mexico City. According to Rogers (2003), "Archives . . . function for those of us in the humanities as laboratories do for our colleagues in the sciences. These are places where we discover new information, test hypotheses, and uncover new fields of study. Undergraduates with sufficient preparation may come to help us in the same way they do in the research labs of our colleagues by making possible more thorough analyses and enabling us to work through larger quantities of data" (p. 134).

Although the type of work undertaken in "research" or even "scholarship" is intuitive to some degree, the work that can be defined as "creative activity" may be so obvious that some may think there is a more complex meaning behind its broad heading. Just as undergraduate research and scholarship comprise a mosaic of academic pursuits, so do undergraduate creative activities. For the sciences, the laboratory is where experiments are run. In the humanities, a student could perform an archival library search on a specific topic. The methods by which these students carry out their research or scholarly work are defined and driven by the discipline. So, too, are the methods and "products" of student artists, musicians, designers, filmmakers, and actors. The blank canvas, sheet music, script, fabric, floor plan, musical instrument, and voice are all examples of the mechanisms these students use to carry out their creative activity.

One need only peruse undergraduate research symposium or conference programs to see the wide range of creative activities that students perform. For example, the 2007 University of Washington Undergraduate Research Symposium featured creative works such as "Elegant Forms in the Everyday" (senior, photography) and "The Birth and Growth of Modern Dance in Seattle: A Look at the Life and Work of Martha Nishitani" (senior, dance, drama). The Southern California Conference for Undergraduate Research included an art exhibit featuring the work of students. The artist described one mixed-medium painting for the 2006 conference as "a depiction of loss and longing for life on the spiritual and physical plane." Another student provided a recording of a live performance of his work "Dracula and the Beanstalk." These few examples show how students in the humanities and performance and visual arts participate in creative activities—the equivalent of research in the natural, physical, and social sciences.

Historical Context of Undergraduate Research and Creative Activities

Historical perspective on undergraduate research and creative activities is related to the evolution of undergraduate curriculum. As Rudolph (1977) noted, the earliest colleges in the New World created their standards and expectations for a curriculum in a vacuum. At the time of their creation, starting with Harvard in 1636 and followed by eight more colleges in the seventeenth and eighteenth centuries, the colonial colleges served a very small population of young men who attended college to learn Greek, Latin, and Hebrew and a few other subjects in a limited curriculum. The primary goal of the curriculum at the time was to prepare these students to be ministers or to inherit the family's wealth (Rudolph, 1990). Other subjects such as mental and moral philosophy were gradually added over time, covering topics well suited to young men aspiring to be ministers but of limited value to less sophisticated vocations.

Modeled loosely after the English undergraduate institutions of Oxford and Cambridge, early American colleges followed the time-honored curriculum prescribed by the *trivium* and the *quadrivium,* a collection of the ancient arts and languages passed down from Greek culture (Rudolph, 1990). The role of faculty and tutors was to convey knowledge in as direct a manner as possible. This effort meant that in most cases, faculty merely passed on the same subject matter they had learned, using the same methods of teaching, memorization, and recitation that they themselves had been subjected to as students. There was little in the way of innovation or creativity. The *Yale Report,* published in 1828, upheld the notion that the mind comprised mental "faculties" that could be exercised only by a conditioned response to specific stimuli. Like in weight training, certain areas of the brain were believed to respond to Latin, others to

Hebrew, and so on. From the Yale faculty point of view, the aspects of their curriculum were designed to stimulate the mind in the most effective way. Because only a very small proportion of college-age population attended college, the need to develop a more creative and challenging set of courses and instruction to attract more students was not an issue at the time (Veysey, 1965).

Nonetheless, there were challenges to the status quo. Intellectually curious young men sought additional education in Europe, especially in Germany, where the concept of the graduate school was active. The concepts of *Lehrnfreiheit* and *Lehrfreiheit,* translated as "freedom to learn" and "freedom to teach," were hallmarks of the German higher education system (Rudolph, 1990). *Lehrfreiheit* meant "the university professor was free to examine bodies of evidence and to report his findings in lecture or published form—that he enjoyed freedom of teaching and freedom of inquiry" (Metzger, 1955, pp. 112–113). *Lehrnfreiheit* meant that students "were free to roam from place to place, sampling academic wares; that wherever they lighted, they were free to determine the choice and sequence of courses, and were responsible to no one for regular attendance; that they lived in private quarters and controlled their private lives" (p. 112). This freedom for professors was necessary to provide opportunities for specialization and development of new ideas that drove the research university.

German higher education embraced the concept of discovery and used this enlightened perspective to drive the rapid advance of scientific research, especially in chemistry and physics (Clark, 1997). Humboldt suggested the "unceasing process of inquiry" (cited in Clark, 1997, p. 246) as a means of learning and teaching in higher education. Students' active involvement in the laboratory was encouraged and spread across Germany to other universities and other laboratories. Teaching through research activity meant that students not only learned faster but also learned the process of discovery through their involvement.

As young American scholars returned from Germany, they brought with them the notions of *Lehrfreiheit, Lehrnfreiheit,* and, to a lesser degree, the Humboldtian interest in the process of inquiry. These young scholars may well have engaged their own undergraduates in the process of research and inquiry. Eventually, research universities became the new engines of discovery and creativity in American society.

As American higher education moved from an elite system of education to mass education in the twentieth century and to near universal access in the late twentieth and early twenty-first centuries (Trow, 1974), the sheer numbers of students enrolled in colleges and universities reached unprecedented heights. The rapid increase in the numbers of students enrolled in undergraduate education meant the likelihood of students' engaging in individual conversations with faculty or even in small groups, for discussion would become difficult, if not impossible, in many higher education settings. American higher education became a very valuable commodity. As the demand for college increased, resources were stretched thin. Because a higher education degree is seen as a requirement for success, the opportunity for undergraduate involvement inside and outside the classroom became limited. Undergraduate research, a golden opportunity for students to engage in the learning process, as Humboldt first suggested in 1810, was constrained by the rapid escalation of the higher education enterprise and the increasing specializations of both faculty and students into narrow fields and tasks.

Students today are expected to find a major field of study quickly, to stick with that choice, and to graduate as quickly as possible. Any distractions from this goal are frowned on academically and penalized monetarily. Many legislatures have ordered state-assisted institutions in the twenty-first century to limit student financial aid and to invoke penalties for those students who do not complete their coursework in a specified time. Changing majors, taking time off from school, or any other complications such as too many hours of work are seen as costly deterrents to graduation. In such an environment, Humboldt's idea of "an unceasing process of inquiry" is difficult to achieve. But at the same time, the lack of student involvement in the learning process, the ultimate goal of undergraduate research, makes the learning process sterile and farther removed from the student. Detached from the learning process, many students, especially in the first year or two, often find higher education a meaningless and vacant experience.

Countering the impersonalization of mass higher education are the smaller classes and opportunities that can be found, even at large research universities, in undergraduate research experiences, honors classes, and small living-learning classes. But the interest in engaging undergraduate students in research grew slowly. The first significant effort was at the Massachusetts Institute of Technology (MIT), where the Undergraduate Research Opportunities Program (UROP) was initiated in 1969. A similar program—the Summer Undergraduate Fellowships—was established in 1979 at the California Institute of Technology (Merkel, 2001). The National Science Foundation (NSF) established a program to encourage undergraduate involvement in research in the early 1980s. Specifically, the program, called Research Experiences for Undergraduates (REU), provided grants for eight to ten undergraduates to work on projects in the NSF's scope of interest (Merkel, 2001).

As these criticisms raised a call for more undergraduate activity in research, a few individuals on several campuses took several steps. The Council on Undergraduate Research was begun in 1978 under the direction of a group of chemistry professors on several liberal arts campuses (Merkel, 2001). The idea grew over time, and in 1987, the first National Conference on Undergraduate Research was held in Asheville, North Carolina, drawing 500 students from a broad range of institutions (Merkel, 2001). The organization, CUR, and the national conference, NCUR, have continued to grow in numbers and influence ever since. The value of undergraduate research has deep roots in American education. The real benefit is the engagement of students with faculty in the process of discovery and learning. To have the benefit of a tutorial experience with faculty in a small group or even one-on-one has long been the ultimate learning experience.

Research activities are now often offered through formalized government-sponsored programs such as the National Science Foundation's REU as well as through institutionally based programs in academic departments or university honors programs. Organizations such as the Howard Hughes Medical Institute (http://www.hhmi.org) or the National Institutes of Health (http://www.nih.gov) sponsor programs in which students participate in research activities. Additionally, disciplinary organizations such as the Conference Experience for Undergraduates offer undergraduate research conference experiences sponsored by various professional and governmental agencies (http://physics.westmont.edu/ceu/). And undergraduate students can publish the findings from the projects they have worked on in academic journals. The appendix includes resources that might be useful for undergraduate students and those who are interested in promoting undergraduate engagement in research and creative activities.

A wide range of activities reflect the spirits of research, inquiry, and creative activities for undergraduate students, although differences exist across and within disciplines. American colleges and universities inherited and expanded the tradition of being "places of inquiry" (Clark, 1995) by engaging undergraduate students in research and creative activities, a trend that has become more noticeable as colleges and universities purposefully devote energy and resources to this innovative strategy in undergraduate education.

Intellectual Foundations of Undergraduate Research and Creative Activities

ENGAGING UNDERGRADUATES IN RESEARCH and creative activities is an intuitively and conceptually appealing approach to improving college students' learning experiences. The idea is a mix of constructivist learning and several well-known educational practices such as experiential learning, problem-based learning, and inquiry-based learning. It also contains long-standing principles of "good practices" in much of the higher education literature. According to Pascarella and Terenzini (2005), "undergraduate research programs are an amalgam of situational and behavioral factors intended both to provide a window on the intellectual life of the scholar and to promote students' active involvement in their own learning, increased and more meaningful interaction with faculty members, opportunities to apply course-related theory and skills in solving real problems, and a challenging intellectual activity" (p. 406).

This section explores the connections between undergraduate research and creative activities with existing theories and exemplary learning models.

Constructivist Learning Theories

A well-known school of thought in student learning is the constructivist framework, exemplified by the work of Bruner (1966, 1985). Based on this framework, knowledge is seen as constructed by learners as they attempt to make sense of their experiences. Individuals' knowledge constructions therefore do not necessarily reflect external reality. Rather, they should be seen as the best construction of experience (Driscoll, 1993). Individuals socially negotiate meanings by testing their own understanding against those of others, especially those of teachers or more advanced peers. From this perspective, the role of teacher and teaching is to help students to discover principles by themselves. The teacher's task is to translate information into a format appropriate to the learner's current state of understanding. Curriculum therefore should be organized in a spiral manner so that students continually build on what they have already learned (Bruner, 1966).

Another influential perspective in the domain of constructive learning theories is scaffolding. Scaffolding is a metaphor that is used to characterize a special type of instructional process that works in a task-sharing scenario involving teacher and learner. From this perspective, a more knowledgeable other plays a necessary role in supporting learning by helping the learner with the aspects of the task that the learner cannot yet manage on his or her own. At the same time, learning occurs when students are challenged to develop new competencies (Vygotsky, 1978).

With this thought in mind, Vygotsky defined an essential feature of learning as the "Zone of Proximal Development" (ZPD), which is "the distance between the actual development level as determined by independent problem-solving and the level of potential development as determined through problem-solving under adult guidance or in collaboration with more capable peers" (p. 86). The ZPD is a region that becomes accessible to the student through the assistance of a more competent peer, teacher, or expert. Some refer to "scaffolding" as specific teacher behaviors in this zone (Bruner, 1985) and claim that "good learning" occurs in the individual's ZPD (Vygotsky, 1978). Learning in this zone with another's help, the learner internalizes the knowledge that is manifested in the interaction. Once the knowledge is internalized, what was the previous potential development level now becomes the new actual development level. Therefore, scaffolding can be seen as a concrete strategy of dynamically locating the individual's shifting ZPD.

Another implication of Vygotsky's notion of the ZPD is the transition from other-regulation to self-regulation. As the teacher's scaffolding is progressively removed, the student performs more independently. Wertsch (1984) described a continuum from other-regulation to self-regulation in terms of expert-novice interaction. He described levels of student performance to illustrate a student's progress in the ZPD. On the first level, the novice is unable to comprehend the problem presented by the expert. On reaching the final level, however, the novice is able to demonstrate complete and independent task mastery. The levels between these two extremes represent a gradual transfer of expertise and responsibility from the expert to the novice.

The constructivist learning theories are particularly useful in understanding the process of undergraduate research and creative activities in student learning. Participation in research and creative activities is beyond the conventional knowledge acquisition and offers undergraduate students an opportunity to maximize their learning in their ZPD. In this learning process, mentoring by the faculty or others serves as scaffolding to aid students' mastery of the skills and transition from other-regulation to self-regulation in knowledge discovery and the learning process.

Exemplary Learning Models

Over decades, learning scientists and educators have proposed various models to enhance student learning outcomes. Following is a brief description of some relevant learning models that have implications for undergraduate research and creative activities.

Experiential Learning

Experiential learning as an educational practice has roots in Dewey's philosophy of pragmatism. Dewey (1997) suggested that individual experience results from the interaction between one's past experiences and the current situation. He argued for the value of learning by doing and the role of reflection, a philosophy congruent with the principle of experiential learning. Accordingly, the role of the educator is to enrich students' experiences that also help students contribute to society.

Kolb is one of the major figures who advanced the theory of experiential learning and advocated for experiential education. He proposed a four-stage learning model: concrete experience, reflective observation, abstract conceptualization, and active experimentation (Kolb, 1984). He particularly pointed out the central role of "experience" in the student learning process, arguing that "knowledge is created through the transformation of experience. Knowledge results from the combination of grasping and transforming experience" (p. 41).

Experiential learning considers students as active agents in the learning process and values students' experiences. Therefore, providing students opportunities to actively engage in the learning process and learning from their experiences is one of the cornerstones in teaching and learning.

Problem-Based Learning

Originated from the education of medical professionals, problem-based learning has become widely used in higher education. It has roots in the tradition of experience-based education. The curriculum in the problem-based learning model utilizes problems or challenges that could be encountered in one's career (Barrows and Tamblyn, 1980). Learners are expected to find solutions to those problems on their own or in small groups, with the instructor as a facilitator. This learning model encourages students to become self-directed in their learning process, to actively engage in knowledge acquisition and problem solving, and to effectively work in a team environment (Barrows and Tamblyn, 1980). The learning process is problem driven and solution oriented, and students acquire knowledge and skills while they seek solutions to the problems. Hmelo-Silver (2004) argues that problem-based learning can help students develop flexible understanding and lifelong learning skills.

Inquiry-Based Learning

Inquiry-based learning is an extension of problem-based learning. It is a student-centered approach that aims to enhance students' skills in questions, problem solving, and critical thinking. Inquiry-based learning emphasizes the importance of involving the student in the discovery of knowledge (Barell, 2006). From the perspective of inquiry-based learning, human beings have innate curiosity about the outside world. Learners in the inquiry-based learning model are not only expected to acquire knowledge but also to identify problems and to discover new knowledge.

One reason that educators, particularly those from the STEM fields, have traditionally used undergraduate research activities in their teaching is that inquiry-based activities enhance the learning process through hands-on experience. During these activities, students apply the skills and knowledge obtained in the classroom or through research experiences to solve open-ended problems (Strassburger, 1995; Seymour, Hunter, Laursen, and Deantoni, 2004). Seago (1992) goes one step farther, pointing out the importance of research and discovery to cognitive processes, memory, and learning. When students formulate their own frameworks of storing, processing, and retrieving information, they are better able to draw from and apply this information to solve problems in a manner meaningful to them (Seago, 1992). Essentially, students construct their own way of learning through research activities. They are encouraged to move beyond superficial "learning" processes such as rote memorization and regurgitation of facts and principles to a more active and constructive mode of learning.

Service Learning

Some practitioners and institutions consider service learning a means for students to learn more about solving real-world problems through relevant hands-on educational experiences while meaningfully contributing to a community (Paul, 2006). Service learning is defined and administered in many different ways. Many academics are skeptical of the educational value of service learning, but some programs have devised ways to incorporate academic rigor by cultivating collaborations between community partners who can navigate the political and social terrain of their communities and academic experts who contribute research design, methodologies, and data analysis (Eyler and Giles, 1999; Paul, 2006). Although service-learning experiences vary in the emphasis on and priority of either the service or the learning component, some educators have introduced programs such as community-based research, which provides service to a community by using and applying higher-order academic skills to identify and address community needs and issues (Paul, 2006).

Community-based research represents a fusion of undergraduate research and service learning, which Paul (2006) describes as "collaborative inquiry that is dedicated primarily to servicing the research or information needs of community organizations" (p. 13). Students in community-based research activities are involved in program evaluation, information gathering for program development, and community needs assessments. At the conclusion of their work, students create and present a report for the organization to use for further planning or decision making.

For both service learning and community-based research, witnessing and identifying the real-life community issues and formulating solutions provide thought-provoking experiences. The reflection component of service learning offers the student a way to connect the new knowledge that was constructed through service learning or community-based research with previous knowledge. Students critically reflect on their experiences through journal entries, reports, questions and answers, or class discussions. Reflection has been consistently linked to outcomes such as reductions in stereotyping, increased tolerance, problem solving, critical thinking, and perspective transformation (Eyler and Giles, 1999).

Implications for Undergraduate Research and Creative Activities

Constructivist learning theories suggest the importance of presenting students with tasks that require knowledge and skills above their current level and the valuable role of mentoring and support of faculty members in this learning process. The exemplary learning models suggest the active role of the students in their own learning process by emphasizing the student-centered nature in knowledge acquisition and discovery of new knowledge. They all point to the potential of undergraduate research and creative activities in contributing to student learning and intellectual development. When students engage in research and creative activities, they will likely be involved in the process of identifying problems to study, designing procedures to find solutions to the problems under study, analyzing information, presenting research findings, and explaining the results. Moreover, an expert, either a faculty member or an advanced graduate student, will likely mentor students' participation in such activities by suggesting opportunities to interact with others intellectually and socially. Those students may develop a sense of community in an intellectually stimulating environment. In sum, student engagement in research and creative activities will likely produce desirable outcomes in undergraduate students.

Understanding Student Engagement in Research and Creative Activities

CONSTRUCTIVIST LEARNING THEORIES and long-standing learning models point to the potential influences of student engagement in research and creative activities. This section uses theories and conceptual models in higher education to understand environmental influences on students' engagement in research and creative activities and to further understand the role of such engagement in students' educational experiences and college outcomes.

Environmental Effects in Higher Education

Higher education researchers consider environment a significant factor in shaping a student's academic and social experiences (Astin, 1993a, 1993b; Tinto, 1975, 1993; Weidman, 1989). One of the best-known models is Astin's input-environment-outcome (I-E-O) model, which was a conceptually parsimonious yet powerful framework in understanding the impact of college on students. The construct of "environment," however, can be defined in various ways. Dimensions of environment often draw from the academic traditions of psychology, sociology, and anthropology. This area of higher education presents a particular challenge, because "environment" comprises many different elements. Indeed, because environmental constructs encompass a broad range of aspects such as students, classes, faculty, facilities, and extracurricular activities, formulating consistent definitions of these dimensions becomes difficult as a result of the varying contexts in which "environment" can be studied.

Baird (1974, 2005) pointed out that defining "environment" then becomes a matter of emphasis and cited how previous studies generally fell into two categories: those that attempted to accurately describe college environments and those that examined college effects. Generally, environment represents the conditions or characteristics existing at various theoretical and organizational levels that influence an individual. Strange (2003) presented four main categories in which environmental models and theories influence an individual's interaction in specific surroundings: (1) design and quality of physical features; (2) shared characteristics of groups of people, also known as human aggregates; (3) influential forces of campus organizational structures and designs; and (4) constructed or perceptual meanings individuals attach to the physical, communal, and organizational aspects of their environments. In the I-E-O model, student outcomes are presumed to be a function of the interactions of inputs and the environment, and "environment" is a broad term that can refer to "the full range of people, programs, policies, cultures, and experiences that students encounter in college, whether on or off campus" (Pascarella and Terenzini, 2005, p. 53). According to this model, student engagement is one of the environmental variables that affect student college outcomes.

Another influential model is Pascarella's general causal model for assessing college impacts on students (1985). In this model, student outcomes are presumed to be a function of the interaction of student background characteristics (inputs), institutional characteristics (size, affluence, student-faculty ratio), student perceptions of the environment, student interactions with agents of socialization (faculty, peers), and student quality of effort (Hu and Kuh, 2003). Institutional environment was explicitly conceptualized as a result of the interaction of student characteristics and institutional characteristics such as organizational or structural features. Further, institutional environment was conceptualized to affect student engagement in college activities, including student interactions with socialization agents such as peers and faculty, and student quality of effort in various activities. Student engagement in those activities then affects student outcomes.

The conceptual approach used in this monograph is a hybrid model following the basic ideas of the I-E-O and the Pascarella models. Different from the I-E-O model, the environment component can be separated into two sets of variables. The first set consists of environmental characteristics such as institutional environment (size and mission), disciplinary environment (major field and disciplinary culture), and other factors. The second set represents students' engagement in research and creative activities in college (Figure 1). This model also simplifies the Pascarella model by combining the factual characteristics of the environment with students' perception of the environment and combining students' interactions and quality of effort as the engagement component of undergraduate research and creative activities. The input component then includes student characteristics such as gender, ethnicity, precollege achievement and aptitude, and other individual characteristics, and the outcomes are cognitive and affective outcomes associated with college education (Astin, 1993a, 1993b; Bloom, 1956; Krathwohl, Bloom, and Bertram, 1973). This treatment maintains the congruence of our model and the well-established models in higher education while it signifies the status of students' engagement in research and creative activities.

FIGURE 1
Guiding Conceptual Framework

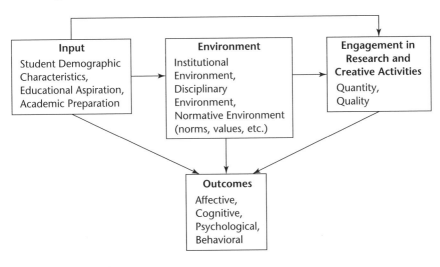

Student Involvement and Engagement

The higher education literature has unequivocally indicated that what matters most in student learning and personal development is what students do in college (Astin, 1985b, 1993a; National Survey of Student Engagement, 2003, 2004, 2005; Pascarella and Terenzini, 1991, 2005). This concept is reflected in Astin's theory of involvement, which essentially suggests that "students learn by becoming involved" (1985a, p. 133). Pascarella adopted Pace's concept of "quality of effort" (1979) in his causal model and signified the importance of students' effort in their own learning and developmental outcomes from college. Chickering and Gamson's *Seven Principles for Good Practice in Undergraduate Education* (1987) continues this line of reasoning. These principles encourage student-faculty contact, cooperation among students, active learning, prompt feedback, time on task, communication of high expectations, and respect for diverse talents and ways of learning. The National Survey of Student Engagement inherited and advanced those ideas by focusing on two frontiers: what students do and what institutions do to help students. The survey and its other related initiatives have brought "student engagement" into the forefront of higher education reform. As important as what students do to their learning, it is also important for institutions to create conditions to engage students and help them get the most out of college (Kuh, Kinzie, Schuh, and Whitt, 2005).

Undergraduate research and creative activities are consistent with the principles in good practices in higher education. For example, the mentor-apprentice dynamic allows for contact between faculty and student, while the research process acts as an active learning experience. The quality of any given research activity may subsequently depend on prompt feedback to students, an emphasis on time on task (the amount of time invested by a student on a particular task and encouragement from the faculty member) and the expectations set by the faculty member.

Engaging students in those activities also exemplifies the concept of "student engagement." As much as students should put forth effort into their own education, college and universities can make a difference by creating opportunities and optimizing the conditions for undergraduate students to participate in research and creative activities. In a study of policies, programs, and practices that various institutions have employed to support student engagement and success, the seven principles formulated by Chickering and Gamson were cited as significant factors in providing high-quality learning environments (Kuh, Kinzie, Schuh, and Whitt, 2005).

The Documenting Effective Educational Practice (DEEP) project examined twenty diverse institutions with strong student engagement and graduation rates and reported the ways these schools provided supportive and engaging environments. With regard to undergraduate research activities, the DEEP report conveyed the importance of providing an academically challenging experience for students coupled with high expectations and appropriate levels of support to facilitate student learning and accomplishment. Some DEEP schools introduced rigor to undergraduate education by requiring senior capstone experiences that ranged from research theses to portfolios to comprehensive examinations (Kuh, Kinzie, Schuh, and Whitt, 2005).

Undergraduate research activities were also highlighted as a way DEEP schools provide active and collaborative learning opportunities for their students. According to students from DEEP institutions, working together with a faculty member on a research project was a highlight of their undergraduate experience and helped foster a better understanding of their professors, deepened their learning, and for some, opened new opportunities beyond college such as graduate school (Kuh, Kinzie, Schuh, and Whitt, 2005).

Undergraduate Socialization

Undergraduate research and creative activities can function not only as effective educational tools but also as ways to socialize students to the culture of their disciplines and as future professionals in their fields. Socialization is an active-learning process in which students acquire skills and knowledge to understand the workings of college life, the importance of a well-rounded academic experience, the sociological imagination, and the ethics and standards of the discipline (McKinney, Saxe, and Cobb, 1998). Professional socialization can be fostered through mentoring relationships, discipline-based student clubs, independent research projects, volunteer service, and informal interactions with faculty members (McKinney, Saxe, and Cobb, 1998). McKinney, Saxe, and Cobb (1998) contend that experiences that offer interpersonal interactions, group membership, and insight into the informal and formal norms of academic life affect students' beliefs and behaviors. The socialization of undergraduates is significant because it prepares students to function as colleagues and leaders and to serve in other professional roles in their given fields. When students are exposed to the norms of their disciplines, they learn what their organizations consider acceptable and important in terms of conduct, priorities, and other affairs.

Weidman's undergraduate socialization model (1989) specifically examines the factors, processes, and outcomes of college student socialization. This model suggests that students enter college with a certain set of characteristics and values, including normative pressures from their parents, employers, peers, and community. These characteristics influence or constrain student choices in the organizational and structural settings of their colleges (Weidman, 1989). Students are exposed to the normative pressures in these settings, which comprise interpersonal interactions, individual processes and development, and the normative order and expectations expressed by an institution's mission and faculty (Weidman, 1989). These elements, when combined with family pressures, result in the student's changing or maintaining certain incoming values (Weidman, 1989). The model suggests that aspects of a student's collegiate experience (academic and social) influence the student's acquisition of skills, knowledge, and attitudes valued by the community of which the student is a member. Weidman (1989) maintained that the academic department provides normative influences because students take more classes in their majors than in any other field.

One of Weidman's early studies examined five nonintellective values: helping others, administrative leadership, financial success, creativity, and career eminence. The results revealed that the academic department influenced student values by discipline type or by faculty-student contact. For example, the humanities (such as English) or social science fields (history or political science) impacted students' interpersonal orientation toward helping others, while student-faculty interaction influenced the career orientation value, career eminence (Weidman, 1979). Therefore, it is important to consider differences in disciplinary environment in understanding students' engagement in research and creative activities.

Academic and Social Integration

The socialization of undergraduates helps cultivate the next generation of leaders and professionals for any given discipline. Socialization also plays a significant role in the integration of students in their departments and on campus. Students who are engaged in educationally purposeful activities are likely to be better integrated academically and socially. The constructs of academic and social integration initially used by Tinto (1975, 1993), though controversial, have been widely tested with particular focus on students' persistence decisions. Tinto's model consisted of six elements that influence persistence decisions. Preentry attributes such as parental education level, race, gender, and precollege academic ability affect the student's initial goals to complete a bachelor's degree at the institution (institutional commitments) (Tinto, 1975, 1993). The student's institutional experiences serve to either integrate or alienate them, which further influences the student's goal of degree completion at the institution.

The final outcome of this process is the effect on the student's decision to persist at or depart from the institution. As two central constructs in Tinto's model, social integration is the result of day-to-day interactions with various members of society, while intellectual integration stems from the sharing of commonly held values with other members of society. As Pascarella and Terenzini (2005) suggest, "Integration is the extent to which the individual shares the normative attitudes and values of peers and faculty in the institution and abides by the formal and informal structural requirements for membership in that community or in subgroups of it" (p. 54). Therefore, student integration, academically or socially, can be considered an intermediate outcome that is the result of student engagement and a precursor of other college outcomes such as persistence and attainment.

Regarding the role of engagement in research and creative activities, decisions about persistence or departure could be influenced by participation or nonparticipation in undergraduate research activities. For example, a student's decision to become involved in undergraduate research activities affects the student's degree of academic and social integration in his or her academic department. Students who are involved in research activities therefore become academically integrated (as measured by grades, for example) and socially integrated through working with a faculty mentor or a laboratory group, which may help retain students and contribute to their intellectual and personal growth. Not only do undergraduate research experiences have the potential to enhance the educational experiences by academically integrating students but these experiences may also promote retention of students by facilitating connections with faculty members and to the institution.

In sum, undergraduates' participation in research and creative activities is a mechanism that can promote students' investment of time and energy in educationally purposeful activities but can also serve as a socialization process for students so that they get accustomed to disciplinary and professional cultures and become more integrated into both the academic and social systems on campus. Colleges and universities have the opportunity to intentionally design policies and programs to engage students in those activities to optimize students' college experiences and maximize learning outcomes.

Impacts of Student Engagement in Research and Creative Activities

THE WEIGHT OF THE EVIDENCE in the higher education literature points to student engagement as the key factor in student learning, personal development, and other desirable outcomes (Astin, 1993a, 1993b; National Survey of Student Engagement, 2003, 2004, 2005; Pascarella and Terenzini, 1991, 2005). This section synthesizes the empirical evidence about the impact of student engagement on research and creative activities. It first documents the evidence of such engagement on a range of desirable outcomes, then examines its influence on special student populations, and finally examines its influence on the faculty members who engage undergraduate students in research and creative projects.

Outcomes of Undergraduate Research Activities

Engagement in research and creative activities during college years is associated with a variety of outcomes in both the cognitive and affective domains (Astin, 1993a, 1993b; Bloom, 1956; Krathwohl, Bloom, and Bertram, 1973). In fact, the evidence from Pascarella and Terenzini's synthesis (2005) suggests that engaging students in undergraduate research and creative activities is "relatively potent" in producing some desirable outcomes (p. 406). The following sections summarize the outcomes influenced by student engagement in research and creative activities.

Improvement in Writing and Communication Skills

Because writing conference papers or articles for publication is a common recommendation for students who participate in undergraduate research programs, one benefit of undergraduate research is improved student writing. Light (2001) reported that many students found research experiences to have a positive influence on their writing. A common experience for students who improved their writing is working in "a one-on-one, mentored research project with a faculty supervisor" (p. 94). Seymour, Hunter, Laursen, and Deantoni (2004) found that improvements in communication skills such as presentation and oral argument were even more substantial. They attributed improved communication skills to individual or group presentations required in undergraduate research activities.

College Experiences

Engagement in undergraduate research and creative activities provides students with a very different learning experience. Those activities "take students out of a classroom setting and put them at the cutting edge of a project" (Light, 2001, p. 97). It is "hard work, yet students praise it as an especially powerful kind of learning experience" (pp. 97–98).

One aspect of the student college experience is student-faculty interaction. It is well accepted that frequent and meaningful interactions between students and faculty are important to learning and personal development (Astin, 1977, 1993b; Bean and Kuh, 1984; Pascarella, 1985; Pascarella and Terenzini, 1979, 1991, 2005; Tinto, 1993). In general, the more contact between students and faculty both inside and outside the classroom, the greater student development and satisfaction (Astin, 1993b). But both the frequency and nature of student-faculty interaction matters in producing desirable outcomes (Kuh and Hu, 2001; Pascarella and Terenzini, 1991). In this regard, undergraduate research and creative activities provide a rich setting for substantive interactions between students and faculty as they work side by side on a research project (Kuh, Kinzie, Schuh, and Whitt, 2005). Indeed, students generally considered such experiences "a highlight of their undergraduate career" (p. 215). Seaman's recent account (2005) of undergraduate residential life cites undergraduate research experiences as one of the ways students make close personal connections with faculty mentors.

Another aspect is students' interaction with their peers. For those undergraduates who engaged in research and creative activities with other students, the interaction with other students and the development of collegiality with their peers can enrich their own educational experiences. As Seymour, Hunter, Laursen, and Deantoni (2004) suggested, such experience "opened up interesting discussions, and underscored the value of discussion as a professional habit. It offered students new and multiple perspectives on their work, and on its problems, and yielded help when needed" (p. 511).

Constructive Learning
Participation in an undergraduate research program led to significant differences in academic functioning, self-concept, and engagement in institutional activities (Jonides, von Hippel, Lerner, and Nagda, 1992). Students reported increased confidence about their abilities to solve problems and gains in critical thinking and problem-solving skills (Seymour, Hunter, Laursen, and Deantoni, 2004).

Satisfaction
Undergraduate students who had substantial collaboration with faculty reported greater gains on cognitive and personal skills and higher levels of satisfaction with their undergraduate education. The benefits increased as the length of collaboration increased (Bauer and Bennett, 2003).

Persistence
Student retention and clarified goals for career options and graduate school attendance, especially among those who are first-generation students or from underrepresented groups, is promoted by undergraduate research experiences (Nagda and others, 1998; Nnadozie, Ishiyama, and Chon, 2001). Gregerman (1999) and Wubah and others (2000) both suggested that participation in research activities increased the retention of minority students.

Motivation and Learning
Students who participated in research programs were more confident in their research ability and more comfortable in the research setting (Swager, 1997). Seymour, Hunter, Laursen, and Deantoni (2004) suggested that undergraduates

who participated in research indicated increased interest and enthusiasm in their fields. Those students also became more independent and more intrinsically interested in learning. Bauer and Bennett (2003) also suggest such experience has greatly enhanced student development in cognitive and personal skills.

Critical Thinking Skills

Using the major field aptitude test score as a measure of student learning and likelihood in proceeding on to professional or graduate school, Ishiyama (2002) found students who majored in political science benefited from their participation in research activities. Eddins and others (1997) and James (1998) contend that participation in undergraduate research makes it more likely that students master complex scientific concepts and develop advanced critical thinking skills. Those skills further benefit students' graduate education (Sakalys, 1984; Peppas, 1981). Volkwein and Carbone (1994) suggest that undergraduate research has a positive impact on undergraduate intellectual growth and personal satisfaction. Bauer (2001) used repeated measures analyses and found that involvement in undergraduate research influenced two college outcomes, critical thinking and reflective judgment.

Academic Achievement

In a study of the relationship between early participation in undergraduate research and student learning in social sciences and humanities at Truman State University, Ishiyama (2002) found that students who reported early participation had greater intellectual gains than those who did not participate. Moreover, early participation in undergraduate research was most beneficial for first-generation college students. The author defined early participation as working with a faculty member on a research project in the freshman or sophomore years.

Enrollment in Graduate School

Using data from an online survey of students from forty-one institutions, Lopatto (2004) found that participants reported a wide range of benefits from their participation in undergraduate research. Gender and ethnic status did not appear to significantly affect the relationship between participation in undergraduate research activities and reported benefits and intent to continue for graduate education (Lopatto, 2004). Bauer and Bennett (2003) also found that students who had substantive research experiences were more likely to enroll in graduate school. Seymour, Hunter, Laursen, and Deantoni (2004) found that undergraduate students who participated in research activities enhanced their preparation for graduate school as a result of their enhanced research experiences and networking opportunities with faculty and professionals. In an evaluation of the NSF's programs related to undergraduate research, Russell (2006) reported that about 40 percent of the participants reported higher expectations for advanced degrees than before their first research experience. Moreover, interest in the Ph.D. increased from 25 percent before undergraduate research experiences to 45 percent after undergraduate research experiences (Russell, 2006). These differences were highest for engineering and life sciences and lowest for physics and mathematics (Russell, 2006).

Choice of Major and Career

Tompkins (1998) argued that students' participation in undergraduate research provided opportunities for female students to pursue science as a career. Similarly, Wasserman (2000) concluded that "hands-on experience in a research laboratory at an early stage persuaded many women to become scientists" (p. 176). Campbell (2002) studied a research program at Texas Tech and concluded that such a program "contributed to the fellow's career success—gained confidence and increased interest in science" (p. 104). Seymour, Hunter, Laursen, and Deantoni (2004) also found that students clarified and refined their educational and career paths because of participation in research activities.

In her evaluation of the NSF's support for undergraduate research opportunities, however, Russell (2006) found that students who entered these experiences with the intent of clarifying future academic or career decisions or for their own personal curiosity and enthusiasm were more likely to be interested in a research career or to pursue a Ph.D. She points out that these findings "suggest that research participation is most likely to be an effective motivator when it is done voluntarily and out of a genuine interest and that requiring research experiences for undergraduates may be counterproductive" (p. 22).

It is evident that participation in research and creative activities has positive effects on a range of desirable outcomes. A recent study by Hu, Kuh, and Li (2007) using College Student Experiences Questionnaire (CSEQ) data, however, suggested that such engagement had positive effects on gains in science and technology, vocational preparation, and intellectual development but had somewhat negative effects on gains in general education and personal development, all other things being equal. For lower-achieving students, no significant relation existed between engagement in inquiry-oriented activities and the gain measures in this study. This finding suggests that there is much more to learn about the nature and quality of undergraduate research and its impact on undergraduate students. One way to foster general education outcomes would be to encourage students to reflect on the implications of their research (whatever the field) for improving the welfare of disadvantaged groups and for strengthening democratic processes. Another step might be to expect students to demonstrate how the results of their research relate to emerging research in other fields. To promote personal development, students could be asked to reflect on how the research process has benefited them personally.

Impacts for Special Student Populations

As mentioned in Tinto's theory, involvement in the academic and social realms of a university helps retain students by integrating them in the institution's culture. Academic and social integration occur when students are involved with peers and faculty members and in extracurricular or cocurricular activities. Background characteristics such as race, ethnicity, academic preparation, socioeconomic status, and overall environment may inhibit integration in either the academic or social spheres, which negatively affects persistence of minority or first-generation students (Loo and Rolison, 1986; Madrazo-Peterson and Rodriguez, 1978). When students feel alienated from an institution's culture, the threat of attrition exists. Minority students' participation in undergraduate research activities may be one way to promote student retention by mediating threats of attrition (Nagda and others, 1998; Nnadozie, Ishiyama, and Chon, 2001).

Extending undergraduate research experiences to honors students is a natural choice, as many of these students are academically high achievers and can generally manage the rigors of research. Undergraduate research experiences have the potential to recruit students into the pipeline of disciplines where they are traditionally underrepresented, however (Kinkead, 2003). Additionally, such experiences can assist in retaining other special populations such as African American men to help foster cognitive and skill development, independence, and personal growth (Kinkead, 2003). Russell (2006) found that among racial and ethnic groups, the effects of research experience (such as understanding the research process, increased confidence in research abilities, awareness of academic and career options) tended to be strongest among Hispanics and weakest among non-Hispanic whites but that most differences between racial and ethnic groups were small. Additionally, there were almost no differences between men and women (Russell, 2006).

Several examples are available of programs that target special populations: the Ronald E. McNair Postbaccalaureate Achievement Program that incorporates research experiences to prepare disadvantaged students with strong academic potential for doctoral studies; the University of Michigan's Undergraduate Research Opportunity Program, which was originally designed to enhance undergraduate education and improve minority student retention; and the Bridge Summer Research Program at the University of California, Los Angeles, which provides research experiences to community college students (http://college. ucla.edu/urc-care/progbridge1.htm). UCLA's program is notable because it is explicitly for community college students. This effort falls in line with the suggestion of the Boyer Commission on Educating Undergraduates in the Research University (1998) that transfer students be integrated in the research environment through special seminars or courses similar to freshman seminars.

Using data collected from the UROP at the University of Michigan, Hathaway, Nagda, and Gregerman (2002) found that research experiences are related to the pursuit of graduate education for underrepresented students of color. The UROP participants were more likely to pursue law, medical, or doctoral degrees. For white and Asian American students, however, undergraduate research participation was not related to the pursuit of graduate education but to the pursuit of professional degrees.

In an evaluation of the NSF's undergraduate research programs (Russell, 2006), students reported a number of positive gains as a result of participating in undergraduate research. Almost all the participants reported gains in understanding, awareness, and confidence about research, graduate school, and careers in STEM fields. More specifically, about 75 percent reported increased interest in a career in STEM fields as a result of participation in research (Russell, 2006). This result was particularly important for Hispanic and Latino participants, who reported the most increase in interest among ethnic groups.

The literature contains a few empirical studies that assessed the effectiveness of institutional undergraduate research programs. Most of the studies focused on educational outcomes associated with participation in undergraduate research, but a few are more specific to programmatic aspects that lead to desired outcomes. In a study that examined the relationship between the rigor of McNair programs and the success of students, Nnadozie, Ishiyama, and Chon (2001) found that the research internship component of McNair programs was the most effective in relation to graduate school placement and admissions. Of particular interest are the findings related to the characteristics, rigor, and impact of the research internship component of the programs in the study. In general, programs had rigorous requirements for entry into the research internship component of the McNair program, but the requirements for completion were not as thorough. The requirements cited most often for the research internship were a proposal and research design, whereas requirements for completion stopped short of presentation of results and publication of findings. The results from this study indicated that rigorous entry requirements and the opportunity to present and publish findings were not a part of all McNair programs; these activities, however, were identified as essential to the success of undergraduate research programs. Similar to Hakim's recommendation (1998), this study supports the notion that undergraduate research programs should incorporate presentations and writing for publication into their design.

Effects on Faculty Members

As undergraduate research and creative activities gain momentum as effective learning tools, more institutions are seeking ways to provide additional opportunities for their students. Students who participate in research activities come away with a plethora of experiences and skills that they will carry with them regardless of what they ultimately decide to do for an occupation or with their education. The tangible dividends for faculty members, however, are relatively small compared with activities that contribute to rewards such as tenure, promotion, and salary increases (Chopin, 2002).

The obvious disparity in benefits for professors can make a difficult case for promoting educational reform efforts such as undergraduate research. Chopin (2002) notes that "the tangible, measurable rewards to the professor are over-shadowed by the personal satisfaction we gain by playing an active role in the personal and professional growth of our students. In effect, we become their intellectual parents" (p. 3). Time is a precious commodity, and faculty members must divide their time wisely to stay current in their fields while also working to advance their careers. As Cech (2003) points out, although undergraduate research activities are "inherently inefficient with respect to faculty effort per student," they are "strikingly effective in their impact on young people's lives" (p. 165).

Nevertheless, faculty must contend with many factors that are finite in nature, and to work with undergraduates as a research or scholarly mentor requires the professor to work around such limitations creatively. For example, undergraduates often lack the necessary experience and basic knowledge to carry out a research project independently. For the professor, this reality means that the student will require more training and supervision than a graduate student employed on the project (Greendyke, 2002). Undergraduate students also require more flexibility with class schedules, more time mentoring and meeting, and more patience as a result of their lack of self-discipline or even maturity (Greendyke, 2002; Howes and others, 2005; Paalman, 2002). The solution provided by Greendyke (2002) entails breaking down a complex project to more achievable parts among undergraduate students. To simplify a project in a way that makes it feasible for a student to complete, however, requires more time and effort on the professor's part. These considerations are an important part of the reality for faculty members who wish to involve undergraduates in research experiences. Mervis (2001) reported that in 1996, faculty members at St. Mary's College of Maryland first voted to require a research-based project of all seniors and started working with students on a voluntary basis. In 2000, the faculty modified the policy to give departments the choice to impose the requirement, citing the difficulty and time-consuming nature of such efforts as well as the lack of preparation by students as reasons for the change (Mervis, 2001).

In making recommendations for strategies for successful undergraduate research experiences, Chopin (2002) first prefaces the steps by advising "know what you are getting into" and notes that "commitment is necessary because mentoring undergraduate researchers is a time-intensive endeavor. The professor must enter into this partnership fully cognizant of these demands and determined to make the time to be a successful mentor" (pp. 7–8). When asked to rate the value of undergraduate research experiences on their professional development, faculty members rated such activities as 3.6 on a nine-point scale (Mervis, 2001). Despite an incentive of a one-course credit for every six projects supervised, many faculty members viewed such activities more as a burden than a benefit (Mervis, 2001).

An often-reported benefit of working with undergraduates is the personal satisfaction of contributing to a student's intellectual and personal development (Chopin, 2002; Russell, 2006). Some contend that by working with undergraduates, faculty are presented with questions in a new light; that is, students ask questions that offer a different perspective or require a faculty member to rethink the approach to a problem (Cech, 2003; Chopin, 2002). Hoopes (1993) points out that although professors who work with undergraduates consequently see slower progress in their research and rate of publications, in some cases, they are able to experiment with high-risk, low-cost projects in an effort to investigate a new area of research. This development occurs because undergraduates are interested in new and unusual ideas and are willing to try new ideas without fear of failure (Hoopes, 1993). Again, the small payoff for professors in working with undergraduates may not be enough to expand such efforts at many institutions, especially research universities. Lopatto of Grinnell College, who partnered with Seymour of the University of Colorado–Boulder in studying the features of "good" research experiences, stated, "The benefits of undergraduate research will be related to a university's commitment" (Mervis, 2001, p. 1614). Although Lopatto may have been referring to student experiences, this statement could be equally true of the faculty members who supervise undergraduates.

As suggested by Elgren and Hensel (2006), undergraduate research and creative activities, done properly, can benefit students in learning and personal development outcomes, can also benefit faculty mentors by expanding their research agenda, and may ultimately contribute to the discovery of knowledge and the advancement of the discipline. The impact of the experience, however, will surely depend on the quality of the relationship between student and faculty member, the length and nature of the research project, the role of the student, and the nature and frequency of feedback the student receives during the endeavor. Thus, there is much more to investigate and learn about the effects of student-faculty research and the characteristics of such collaborative efforts that make for a productive, rewarding activity for both partners.

What Matters to Student Engagement in Research and Creative Activities

PARTICIPATION IN RESEARCH AND CREATIVE ACTIVITIES
enriches undergraduate educational experiences and promotes a variety of
desirable outcomes. The evidence of the research to date lends support to the
advocacy of engaging students in research and creative activities as a pathway
to reinvigorate undergraduate experiences in the United States. To develop
effective programs, however, it is necessary to identify the patterns of student
engagement in those activities and to distill the factors related to such student engagement. This section first demonstrates the patterns of student
engagement in research and creative activities using data from the National
Survey of Student Engagement (NSSE) and the College Student Experience
Questionnaire research programs. It then discusses the correlates of student
engagement in research and creative activities.

Patterns of Student Engagement

Although an important indicator of the quality of undergraduate education,
the extent to which undergraduate students participate and engage in research
and creative activities has not been well documented. Fortunately, more recent
national surveys on college students have corrected this deficit and offer opportunities to empirically describe the patterns of student participation and
engagement in research and creative activities. In a recent study, Hu, Kuh,
and Gayles (2007) used longitudinal data from the CSEQ research program
at Indiana University to compare the frequency of student participation in

FIGURE 2
Research Experience Composite by Institutional Type and Time

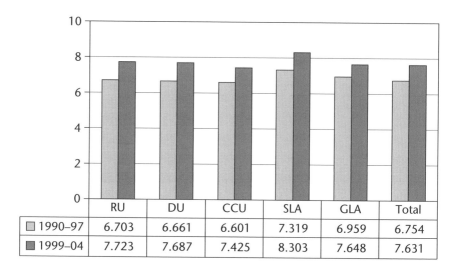

	RU	DU	CCU	SLA	GLA	Total
▢ 1990–97	6.703	6.661	6.601	7.319	6.959	6.754
▪ 1999–04	7.723	7.687	7.425	8.303	7.648	7.631

Note: RU = Research Universities, DU = Doctoral Universities, CCU = Comprehensive Colleges and Universities, SLA = Selective Liberal Arts Colleges, GLA = General Liberal Arts Colleges.

research and creative activities from the early 1990s through 2004 (Figures 2 and 3). In the CSEQ, students were asked to respond to the following items: "worked with a faculty member on a research project," "discussed ideas for a term paper or other class project with a faculty member," "gone back to read a basic reference or document that other authors referred to," and "completed an experiment or project using scientific methods." The response options for these items were 1 = never, 2 = occasionally, 3 = often, and 4 = very often. Hu, Kuh, and Gayles (2007) examined both students' responses to the one question on working with a faculty member on a research project and the composite scores of all items as an overall indicator. They reached the following conclusions:

1. Even though research universities are best known for their inquiry-intensive missions—and indeed many research universities feature opportunities to work side by side with productive scholars in their recruitment

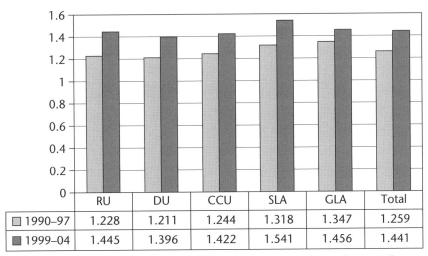

	RU	DU	CCU	SLA	GLA	Total
▨ 1990–97	1.228	1.211	1.244	1.318	1.347	1.259
▧ 1999–04	1.445	1.396	1.422	1.541	1.456	1.441

Note: RU = Research Universities, DU = Doctoral Universities, CCU = Comprehensive Colleges and Universities, SLA = Selective Liberal Arts Colleges, GLA = General Liberal Arts Colleges.

materials and institutional Web sites—students at research universities were not more likely than their counterparts elsewhere to have experiences in research and creative activities.

2. The frequency of student research experiences increased at all types of institutions and across all disciplines since 1998, the year when the Boyer Commission on Educating Undergraduates in the Research University released its national report calling for an inquiry-based undergraduate education. This trend is consistent with Katkin's assessment (2003) on the impact of the Boyer report. The result suggests that the calls for improving undergraduate education by encouraging students to work with faculty on research activities may be having the intended effects.

Recent data from the NSSE were used to further describe the patterns of student participation and engagement in undergraduate research and creative activities. The analysis revealed the following patterns (Table 1):

TABLE 1
Percentages of Students Who Participated in Research Activities with Faculty

	First-Year Students		Seniors	
	No	Yes	No	Yes
Gender				
Male	95.5%	4.5%	76.7%	23.3%
Female	96.0%	4.0%	79.0%	21.0%
Total	95.8%	4.2%	78.2%	21.8%
Race/Ethnicity				
African American	94.3%	5.7%	79.8%	20.2%
American Indian	95.1%	4.9%	74.8%	25.2%
Asian	96.3%	3.7%	77.2%	22.8%
White	96.1%	3.9%	78.2%	21.8%
Hispanic	94.3%	5.7%	80.1%	19.9%
Other	94.8%	5.2%	78.1%	21.9%
Foreign	93.9%	6.1%	71.5%	28.5%
Multiracial/Ethnic	97.8%	2.2%	81.6%	18.4%
Unknown	95.8%	4.2%	78.2%	21.8%
Total	95.8%	4.2%	78.2%	21.8%
Primary Major Field				
Arts	96.0%	4.0%	78.2%	21.8%
Biological Science	94.9%	5.1%	56.7%	43.3%
Business	96.0%	4.0%	88.5%	11.5%
Education	95.6%	4.4%	86.1%	13.9%
Engineering	95.6%	4.4%	71.0%	29.0%
Physical Science	95.0%	5.0%	56.7%	43.3%
Professional	96.1%	3.9%	81.8%	18.2%
Social Science	96.4%	3.6%	72.4%	27.6%
Other	95.1%	4.9%	81.4%	18.6%
Undecided	97.2%	2.8%	80.0%	20.0%
Total	95.8%	4.2%	78.2%	21.8%
Institutional Control				
Public	96.0%	4.0%	81.2%	18.8%
Private	95.7%	4.3%	75.2%	24.8%
Total	95.8%	4.2%	78.2%	21.8%

TABLE 1 (*Continued*)

	First-Year Students		Seniors	
	No	Yes	No	Yes
Institutional Selectivity				
Noncompetitive	95.3%	4.7%	83.2%	16.8%
Less Competitive	94.5%	5.5%	82.3%	17.7%
Competitive	95.3%	4.7%	81.9%	18.1%
Competitive Plus	95.0%	5.0%	75.2%	24.8%
Very Competitive	96.2%	3.8%	76.3%	23.7%
Very Competitive Plus	96.9%	3.1%	75.8%	24.2%
Highly Competitive	97.3%	2.7%	73.2%	26.8%
Highly Competitive Plus	96.1%	3.9%	63.7%	36.3%
Most Competitive	96.4%	3.6%	66.9%	33.1%
Total	95.8%	4.2%	78.2%	21.8%
Institutional Type				
Doctoral–Extensive	96.8%	3.2%	78.2%	21.8%
Doctoral–Intensive	95.3%	4.7%	80.3%	19.7%
Master's	95.8%	4.2%	81.2%	18.8%
Baccalaureate–Liberal Arts	96.4%	3.6%	67.9%	32.1%
Baccalaureate–General	94.6%	5.4%	80.4%	19.6%
Other	94.6%	5.4%	81.3%	18.7%
Total	95.8%	4.2%	78.2%	21.8%

Source: Calculation from 2005 National Survey of Student Engagement data.

1. The proportion of undergraduate students who participated in research activities with faculty was relatively small for first-year students. The highest was for foreign students at 6.1 percent and the lowest for multiracial and multiethnic students at 2.2 percent, with participation rates for students of other characteristics or in other circumstances in between. Participation rates increased substantially for senior students contrasted with first-year students, however. Participation rates for seniors ranged from 11.5 percent for students in the business fields to 43.3 percent for students in biological and physical sciences.

2. Student participation rates in research activities varied, depending on student characteristics, major fields, and institutional characteristics. Gender

differences appeared to be very small. Regarding students' racial or ethnic background, foreign students had the highest participation rates during both the first year and the senior year, while multiracial and multiethnic students had the lowest participation rates.

3. Students in biological and physical sciences had the highest participation rates, while undecided students had the lowest rate in the first year and business students in the senior year.

4. Students in private institutions had slightly higher participation rates in the first year but much higher rates in the senior year. Students in less competitive institutions appeared to have higher participation rates in the first year but lower participation rates in the senior year. Finally, baccalaureate–liberal arts colleges stood out in terms of participation rates for senior students, with the highest participation rate (32.1 percent). Consistent with previous studies (for example, Hu, Kuh, and Gayles, 2007), the participation rates in research universities were essentially comparable with students in other types of institutions, with the exception of baccalaureate–liberal arts schools in the senior year.

In 2005, the National Science Foundation contracted with the SRI International to evaluate several undergraduate research programs. The study randomly surveyed participants of NSF awards during the 2002–03 academic year and the 2002 summer programs, including Research Experiences for Undergraduates Sites and Supplements, Research in Undergraduate Institutions, NSF-sponsored research centers that included a significant undergraduate research component, the Louis Stokes Alliance for Minority Participation, the Historically Black Colleges and Universities Undergraduate Program, the Tribal Colleges and University Program, Grants for Vertical Integration of Research and Education in Mathematical Sciences, and the Department of Energy programs. The findings supported the outcome that 53 percent of the participants were women and about 40 percent of the participants were minorities. This finding is especially important considering that women and minorities are typically underrepresented in the STEM fields (Russell, 2006). The study found that the undergraduate participants had reasonably good grades (85 percent with a 3.0 or better grade point average), and about 70 percent reported having prior undergraduate research experience (Russell, 2006). Additionally, most of the participants were seniors and attended research universities.

Regarding types of activities undergraduates participated in, more than 80 percent of undergraduates reported that they produced a final report, collected and analyzed data, and understood how their work contributed to the bigger picture (Russell, 2006). Sixty-five percent and 77 percent of undergraduates reported being involved in designing the project and gaining increased independence, respectively, and 35 percent and 47 percent of undergraduates reported going on a research-related field trip and attending a professional conference, respectively (Russell, 2006).

Correlates of Student Engagement

Identifying the characteristics of students who participate in undergraduate research activities is not so straightforward. According to Strassburger (1995), "Faculty often are in awe that so many different students from so many different backgrounds can be led to do substantial work. For faculty, the reminder is that most students can work hard and become engaged, and are capable of a remarkable amount of learning" (p. 5). An additional consideration is that because programs are created and implemented with different objectives, they tend to engage a wide range of students in research and creative activities. Studies and programs ranged from retention of underrepresented students (for example, the Ronald E. McNair Program) to talented students (Kardash, 2000) or included alumni feedback (Bauer and Bennett, 2003; Siebert, 1988), while community college students have been included in research enterprises at their transfer schools or two-year colleges (for example, the multi-institutional Modular Neutron Array [MoNA] project). Studies examining specific personal characteristics of students who participate in research activities are noticeably absent.

One notable exception to this observation is a report generated by the Stanford Research Institute. From 2003 to 2005, the SRI conducted a series of surveys of undergraduate research program participants (students, graduate and postdoctoral mentors, faculty, and alumni) to assemble a more thorough report of undergraduate research experiences. Although the SRI report is largely focused on NSF programs, it offers a closer look at the participants and their motivations, experiences, and characteristics. Among its results, the SRI reported that students from underrepresented populations were "well represented among NSF undergraduate researchers in 2002–2003" (Russell, 2006, p. 5). This finding is not surprising, considering that some NSF undergraduate research programs are specifically geared toward the inclusion of or toward encouraging the participation of women, black, and Hispanic students, especially in the STEM fields. Additionally, the profile of undergraduate researchers described students who were likely to be upper-classmen (juniors and seniors), high achievers with high grade point averages, and students who planned to pursue a doctoral degree (Russell, 2006). The SRI surveys also captured information from non-NSF-sponsored researchers and nonresearch participants to compare NSF-sponsored participants. The SRI information on nonresearch participants provides insight into certain reasons why some students do not take part in research opportunities. Unfortunately, the qualitative differences between student researchers and nonresearchers have not been fully explored or determined by any existing study.

Students appeared to pursue undergraduate research and creative activities for more pragmatic and extrinsic reasons. Some cited their curiosity about research, while others planned to go to graduate school and needed letters of recommendation or wanted to prepare themselves more sufficiently (Russell, 2006; Seymour, Hunter, Laursen, and Deantoni, 2004). An important point that Russell (2006) made is that "participation in undergraduate research seems most likely to have positive outcomes (e.g., increased confidence in one's abilities, interest in a STEM-related career, expectations of obtaining a Ph.D.) if it is done voluntarily and out of genuine interest; research that is done because it is required is less likely to lead to positive outcomes" (p. 26). In short, different students are motivated by different factors to do research. This fact, combined with available institutional support, accounts for the wide array of students who participate in hands-on research activities. The study of the personal characteristics of these students could further enhance the overall information base on undergraduate research.

Undergraduate research experiences can also serve as professional socializing agents for students by exposing them to the values and culture of the academic unit (Seymour, Hunter, Laursen, and Deantoni, 2004). The extent to which students are involved with faculty members can provide a deeper sense of disciplinary norms and values and influence students' career choices and aspirations (McKinney, Saxe, and Cobb, 1998; Weidman, 1989). For example, Weidman's study (1979) found that departmental faculty normative influences on students tend to outweigh the normative influences of peers, especially with respect to career eminence. As students move farther along in the educational process, they tend to find that faculty members are more significant than peers as career role models and as sources of authoritative information about prospective career roles (Weidman, 1979).

Studies report that the level of faculty research orientation affects student outcomes (Astin, 1993b; Pascarella and Terenzini, 1991; Volkwein and Carbone, 1994). Astin's study (1993b) reveals that faculty research orientation has strong correlations with involvement of undergraduates in faculty research ($r = .74$) despite strong negative correlations with student development ($r = -.72$) in self-reported areas such as leadership and growth in public speaking. Other studies, however, report that students experience personal gains in self-confidence, oral and written communications, and emotional growth as a result of being involved in undergraduate research (Lanza and Smith, 1988).

Despite the negative correlations between faculty research orientation and student development, the benefits specifically associated with students' involvement in research activities have been cited in studies where students and alumni report perceived gains of undergraduate participation (for example, Bauer and Bennett, 2003; Wray, 2000). Further, Astin's study (1993b) indicates that strong faculty research orientation facilitates students' participation in educationally purposeful activities (such as students' involvement in a professor's research project). Braxton, Eimers, and Bayer (1996) report faculty members view cognitive development, not affective development, to be their primary goal, which may account for the negative effects on personal development reported in Astin's study. Therefore, faculty involvement in student learning through research activities may be more consistent with faculty roles and responsibilities and beneficial to student educational outcomes.

Volkwein and Carbone (1994) studied departmental climates created by faculty teaching and research activities and the subsequent impact on and student growth and satisfaction. Departments were classified as having various levels of teaching or research orientations (high, moderate, or low) based on measures such as student ratings, grant applications and awards, or a dean's assessment of department research and scholarship. This study revealed that students in departments with balanced research and teaching orientations were more academically integrated; that is, they saw more gains in intellectual growth and disciplinary skills. Interestingly, students in departments with high research and low teaching orientations reported more growth than those in exclusively teaching-oriented departments (Volkwein and Carbone, 1994). These findings, as the authors point out, contradict criticisms that research interferes with teaching. The results of Volkwein and Carbone's study also revealed that research and teaching were independent activities with little to no correlation with one another. The outcomes of their study, however, did not report the results by specific discipline or enumerate the types of academic activities in which students were involved. Such information would be helpful in understanding disciplinary differences in research orientations and their impact on students.

Differences in institutional type, resources, culture, and mission could all affect student engagement in research and creative activities. Using data from the College Student Experience Questionnaire, Hu, Kuh, and Gayles (2007) found that research universities do not provide advantages to undergraduate students in research and creative activities, despite a strong institutional mission of research. Research results from the National Survey of Student Engagement at Indiana University (2003, 2004, 2005) suggest that students at liberal arts colleges are more likely to engage in research and creative activities. This finding may partially explain the disproportionate share of Ph.D. recipients with institutional origins from liberal arts colleges. According to Zimmer (2005), liberal arts colleges enroll only 8 percent of all four-year-college students. More than 17 percent of all Ph.D.'s awarded in science from 1991 to 1995, however, received undergraduate education in liberal arts colleges. Some suggested that faculty members at liberal arts colleges "have an incentive to hook students early and keep them interested in doing research" (Zimmer, 2005, p. B5) because of the lack of graduate students on such campuses.

Program features also matter to student experiences with research activities. Russell (2006), in her evaluation of the NSF programs, reported that undergraduates' perceptions about their experiences were positive overall, with participants reporting different levels of satisfaction for various program components. About 96 percent of participants reported that they were satisfied with the overall experience. More than two-thirds reported that they were satisfied with the mentoring experience and the level of independence in doing their work. A little less than half of the participants were satisfied with the level of involvement in designing and selecting their project.

Key aspects of the research program were of particular importance to participants, including time spent with the faculty mentor, amount and quality of research activities, involvement in designing the project and decision making, and preparation for carrying out various research-related tasks. Students reported that the best parts of the research experience were doing real research, interacting with faculty, being a part of a team, and learning how to figure things out on their own. The worst aspects of the experience were downtime, things not going right, academic politics, unpredictability of research, and interaction with others.

Student engagement in research and creative activities can be influenced by a variety of factors such as student, disciplinary, and institutional characteristics. The real challenge—and opportunity—for colleges and universities is to ensure that students of different backgrounds have equal opportunities to engage in such activities while maximizing such engagement by all students.

Engaging Students in Research and Creative Activities

A S A RESULT OF DIFFERENCES in institutional mission, history, culture, and resources, it is common for institutions to set their own standards for undergraduate research participation. Despite the varied nature of the programmatic structure of undergraduate research programs across the country, the literature suggests key elements of effective programs. This section briefly describes the phases of undergraduate research experiences, then presents some exemplary programs in undergraduate research and creative activities and discusses the conditions and barriers conducive to student engagement in research and creative activities.

Phases of Student Research Experience

The total experience of an undergraduate research activity can be divided into three phases: beginning, middle, and end. The beginning phase involves the requirements for participation in undergraduate research. Requirements set the tone for the overall experience and prepare participants for what lies ahead. Some institutions have seminars for freshmen and sophomores that prepare them for participation in research in the junior and senior years. Preparation to carry out the research is essential to the success of any program. Other programs require students to write a research proposal—a good exercise that gives students some independence and autonomy in selecting a problem to study. Originality of the proposal, as defined by Hakim (1998), should be part of the evaluation and selection criteria for participation.

The middle of the research experience represents the heart of student involvement, marked by the opportunity to engage in conducting research alongside a faculty member. Engagement opportunities include experiences such as writing literature reviews, collecting and analyzing data, and participating in workshops and field trips. Key characteristics of the middle phase of the undergraduate research experience should consist of faculty mentoring and practicing methods of inquiry specific to the field of study. A final product such as a conference presentation or a manuscript submitted for publication marks the end of the research experience. It is imperative that the final product be produced and disseminated in a way that contributes to the conversation in the respective field of study.

Institutional Efforts to Engage Students in Research and Creative Activities

Existing literature has demonstrated that student engagement in research and creative activities has desirable impacts on student learning and personal development (Council on Undergraduate Research and National Conference for Undergraduate Research, 2005; Pascarella and Terenzini, 2005). Colleges and universities have embraced the idea of engaging undergraduate students in research and creative activities and are making further strides in this direction (Hu, Kuh, and Gayles, 2007; Karukstis and Elgren, 2007; Katkin, 2003).

Liberal Arts Colleges

In addition to efforts in academic departments, many liberal arts colleges provide good examples of how those colleges provide students opportunities in research and creative activities.

Harvey Mudd College (HMC) in California is a private college with a strong reputation in math, science, and engineering education. The college has a traditionally integrated research experience in undergraduate education and prides itself as a "grad school for undergrads" (Harvey Mudd College, 2007). The college has purposefully established connections with industry and secures sponsorships from industry to support student research endeavors through its Clinic Program. The Clinic Program was founded in 1963 as an innovative practice in engineering education and now has entered other departments throughout the college. Through the program, juniors and seniors work on real-world problems with the sponsorship of industrial clients (Harvey Mudd College, 2007). Annually, HMC organizes a Presentations Day to showcase students' achievements in the Clinic Program and other research activities, with audiences from both inside and outside the college. The college also sponsors a multidisciplinary journal, *Interface,* to disseminate HMC student research. In 2005, HMC initiated a new Global Clinic Program through which HMC students team up with students from partnering schools in other continents on research projects. Students in the Global Clinic Program receive intensive language instruction and cultural immersion to become prepared for the collaborations with students from other locations and cultures.

Grinnell College in Iowa is another liberal arts college that has often been recognized as an example of engaging undergraduates in research and creative activities. The college established the Mentored Advanced Project (MAP) to encourage students to work with a faculty mentor in conducting research and creative activities. According to the college, "A MAP can be the capstone of the academic major or a concentration, or it can serve to integrate a separate sequence not recognized as a formal program. The MAP may be independent, conducted with a research team, or developed in the context of an advanced seminar" (Grinnell College, 2007). MAP can be taken during the regular semester or during the summer. The college provides students extensive information on opportunities for presentation and publication of the results from their activities and provides funding support for students to present off campus.

Through a grant from the Fullerton Foundation, Wofford College in South Carolina created a ten-week summer program in which up to twenty students selected as research fellows undertake scholarly work in a number of disciplines, from the humanities and social sciences to the traditional sciences. Research fellows work under the supervision of a faculty mentor. Together, this collaboration represents Wofford College's Community of Scholars, whose goals include fostering critical thinking skills and developing the culture of the exchange of ideas between peers and colleagues. During the course of the program, students report their progress at weekly lunches and dinners. During the fall term, students make a formal presentation of their results before a public audience.

Hope College in Michigan provides students with opportunities in creative activities. Many of the arts-based disciplines at Hope involve students in the applied skills of their areas. For example, the college provides opportunities for students in the dance program to learn about choreography, performance, and production through student-produced concerts. Students are responsible for auditioning the cast, selecting wardrobe, and designing lighting for their concert. In addition, every year the faculty of the dance department produce their own concerts. Freshmen are exposed early to performance and related work, as they are required to perform in one student dance concert during their freshman year.

Faculty members are also active in their disciplines. They audition, cast, and choreograph productions in which students may participate. All disciplines in the department are represented (ballet, jazz, tap, and modern). Similarly, theater students at Hope College learn about various aspects of their disciplines through internships offered in locations such as Chicago, Philadelphia, and New York. Through these internships, students get experience in the field by working in positions ranging from backstage work to learning behind-the-scenes technical and design skills to serving as apprentices to active performing artists.

Various other liberal arts colleges create opportunities for their students—whether in science and engineering or in the humanities, arts, and social sciences—to engage in research and creative activities. Some schools use connections with outside sponsors, some secure funds from state or federal government programs to support student endeavors, and others allocate institutional resources to programming. These institutional efforts help enrich students' collegiate experiences.

Research Universities

Even though research universities as a whole do not compare favorably with some selective liberal arts colleges in terms of engaging students in research and creative activities, many well-known institutional programs in undergraduate research and creative activities are housed in research universities.

The Undergraduate Research Opportunities Program at the Massachusetts Institute of Technology was conceived in 1969 and is one of the nation's earliest programs to use research activities as an educational tool for undergraduates. All MIT students in good academic standing are eligible to participate in the program. Students from nearby Wellesley College and the University of Cambridge are also permitted to participate in the UROP under the terms of their respective exchange programs. Students apply for research positions by submitting research proposals to the UROP, which UROP coordinators review. The faculty and academic units are active participants and supporters of the UROP. Each department at MIT has a faculty member who serves as a UROP coordinator, working with students and faculty, evaluating the academic rigor of the project being proposed, and being involved in decisions about financial awards. Students at MIT have the option to select the type of compensation they receive for their research projects. Students have several "participation modes" to choose from:

1. *Academic credit:* Students receive general credit for work completed through the UROP.
2. *Supervisor funding:* Students may approach faculty members about receiving pay from faculty grants. The UROP specifies that the rate of pay must be at least equal to the UROP's hourly rate.
3. *Direct UROP funding:* UROP has limited funding to support hourly pay for student researchers or provide a total stipend.
4. *Volunteer work:* Students volunteer without receiving academic credit or pay and without rigid commitments to research a project. Students applying for volunteer UROP experiences are still required to submit a research proposal.

The University of Michigan's UROP began in 1989 as an institutional initiative to improve retention and academic achievement of underrepresented students. The university's program targets incoming freshmen and second-year students but has provisions to include continuing UROP students and juniors and seniors seeking research experiences. Transfer students, underrepresented students of color, and women are specifically encouraged to apply. Michigan faculty can list current research positions with the UROP and can sponsor students from the UROP pool for a research experience. Additionally, faculty members can apply for supplementary funding. The UROP recognizes the contributions of its faculty sponsors at a spring faculty reception and rewards those who are nominated and selected for their exceptional work with outstanding mentorship awards. Students select their modes of compensation: academic credit or work-study funding. In either instance, students have requirements that they must meet for their research experience: working six to ten hours on a research project, attending UROP research seminars, completing reading and journal assignments for seminars, meeting monthly with their respective peer advisors, and completing an end-of-term project for the fall and winter terms. The UROP also offers sponsored summer fellowships for students that provides laboratory and community-based research experiences under the supervision of a university faculty member and a stipend for their summer work. UROP summer fellows present their summer research findings during a forum in the fall. A summer internship database is also maintained as an option for students seeking experiences related to their academic and career goals.

In addition to opportunities in the traditional science and engineering fields, many efforts have been made to provide opportunities in the humanities and social sciences. Washington University in St. Louis offers an international undergraduate research program in its School of Business. The program targets second-semester juniors to study abroad in France, Germany, and the United Kingdom. The program stands out in that students participate in an intense academic preparation course the semester before travel as well as during study abroad. During the research experience abroad, students are required to write an original research paper under the guidance of a faculty member and present the findings of their research to a panel of faculty, internship supervisors, and student participants. Program participants are highly involved in research activities such as developing the research topic, preparing literature reviews, and collecting and analyzing data. Participation in the international research program is competitive; students are required to submit applications and curriculum vitae. The selection committee is interested in and bases its decisions on students' career interests and previous work experience as well as their academic background.

At Florida State University (FSU), student engagement in the humanities and social sciences was highlighted in the university's recent effort to enrich student experiences in research and creative activities. After exploratory work by the provost's task force on undergraduate research and creative activities, FSU formally established the Office of Undergraduate Research and Creative Endeavors in

2007. This office is charged with coordinating the university's effort to strengthen and develop research opportunities for undergraduate students. One component of the university's effort is its program in humanities, a six- to nine-credit program designed to "introduce high-achieving sophomores, juniors, and seniors to research in the different humanities areas; and . . . to offer these students a hands-on experience of doing research in one of these areas" (Florida State University, 2007, p. 1). The program is competitive and offers opportunities to up to twenty undergraduate students in the first year. Admitted students enroll in a three-credit Interdisciplinary Research Seminar in the Humanities and one other three-credit course in any humanities area during the fall semester. During the spring semester, students who have successfully completed the fall program are eligible to apply for a paid position as an undergraduate research assistant to a faculty member, and they can compete for small research grants to support their own research projects. Students are also encouraged to present their research at the FSU Undergraduate Research and Creativity Symposium, held annually at the end of the spring semester (Florida State University, 2007).

The University of South Florida also offers initiatives for students in the humanities and social sciences. Two such initiatives are the Humanities REU and the Social Aspects of Hurricanes REU, "interdisciplinary programs that combine course work and group training in research skills to prepare cohorts of skilled undergraduate research apprentices" (Yavneh and Ersing, 2007). Students take the necessary coursework to enhance their research skills; they also receive a modest scholarship to support their scholarly activities.

Some research universities have a long tradition of engaging undergraduate students in research and creative activities. Other institutions have intensified their efforts to create new opportunities. Many such efforts try to balance the needs of undergraduate students in different disciplines and institutional efforts to serve as catalysts for further opportunities for undergraduate research and creative activities.

Other Types of Colleges and Universities
Even though liberal arts colleges and research universities receive the most attention in undergraduate research initiatives, many other types of institutions have notable programs in undergraduate research and creative activities.

For example, the Center for Undergraduate Research at Xavier University of Louisiana promotes and provides support for faculty and students to pursue research and other scholarly activities inside and outside the university. Undergraduates at Xavier University have the opportunity to work with faculty mentors at Xavier as well as faculty at other institutions, industry partners, government agencies, and various for-profit and nonprofit organizations. The center receives funding from a variety of sources, including the university and the state. The center has been very successful in writing grants for federal dollars and garnering support from private foundations. Xavier faculty staff the center with one full-time director and two associate directors. The Center for Undergraduate Research offers a number of services and activities for both faculty and students, including workshops for students on topics ranging from how to present a poster session to expectations for the research experience. The center is also instrumental in helping students identify opportunities for research during the summer. Faculty at Xavier may also receive support from the center through a series of workshops and seminars on integrating teaching and research, mentoring, acquiring funding, and writing successful proposals. In addition to services provided, the center sponsors a two-day research forum for faculty and students to present the results from their scholarly and creative activities using a variety of media such as posters, presentations, debates, panels, performances, and demonstrations. The center also publishes an online undergraduate research journal in which students can publish the findings from their work. The online format allows students to post images, video clips, and audio files.

The University of Central Florida (UCF), as a participating institution of the Carnegie Academy for the Scholarship of Teaching and Learning (CASTL), offers a wide range of opportunities for undergraduate students to engage in research and creative activities. The programs geared toward undergraduate students include Honors in the Majors, McNair Scholars program, Research and Mentorship, Undergraduate Research Initiatives, Student-Mentor Academic Research Teams, LEAD Scholars, and Research Experiences for Undergraduates. These different programs have different targeted student populations and requirements. For instance, the LEAD Scholars program targets freshmen and sophomores, REU juniors and seniors, and Undergraduate Research Initiatives all students (University of Central Florida, 2007).

Although research is not traditionally emphasized in community colleges, many have found ways to engage students in research and creative activities (Perez, 2003). The Community College of Southern Nevada was featured in the American Chemical Society's *Chemical and Engineering News* for the work of a chemistry professor who not only works with any student who is interested in doing research but also brings students to professional meetings to present posters of their work. Also featured in the article are the efforts of a professor at Harold Washington College (Chicago), who is the principal investigator on an NSF grant that provides research opportunities to students at ten community colleges and three baccalaureate-granting schools in the metropolitan area. Perez (2003) described a group of community colleges in the "Beacon Associate Colleges" organized to provide venues for their students to showcase their achievements in research.

Engaging undergraduate students in research and creative activities is not just an idea; it has become an increasingly important practice in all types of postsecondary institutions. The diversity of programs and practices in different types of institutions exemplifies institutional efforts to create "conditions that matter" to students' success (Kuh, Kinzie, Schuh, and Whitt, 2005).

Multi-institutional Efforts

Innovation and Collaboration Enhance Physics Undergraduate Education: Meet MoNA is a multi-institutional collaboration to engage undergraduate students in research activities. Research in some areas of physics is often collaborative: groups of scientists gather to run experiments at large facilities and make decisions regarding the direction of experiments and the design of the facilities during group meetings (Howes and others, 2005). Faculty members from predominantly undergraduate institutions typically travel to large research facilities to participate in experiments and group meetings, thus leaving undergraduates with little or no exposure to significant experiences with physics research. A group of physicists from several colleges and universities, recognizing the importance of hands-on experiences for educational purposes and the need to sustain the field of physics with new talent by recruiting graduate students, started the Modular Neutron Array collaboration to provide a solution to this conundrum faced by physics departments at smaller colleges and universities.

With more than $900,000 from the NSF, students from ten colleges and universities from around the country representing a broad spectrum of institutions were able to participate in building a neutron detector to be installed at the National Superconducting Cyclotron Laboratory (NSCL) at Michigan State University (Feder, 2005; Howes and others, 2005). Coordinators of the MoNA effort must ask themselves several important questions as they establish objectives of the program (Baumann and others, 2007):

How can students be continually involved in the forefront of research?

What are the benefits to the students from this participation?

What are the benefits to the institutions and faculty members?

When students participate in the experiments and they work with the datasets, how can they evolve from passive watchers to active doers with the responsibility of finding answers?

Students involved in building the neutron detector were given an integral component of the detector to assemble and calibrate that was eventually sent and installed at the NSCL. These students, who were supervised by one or two professors from their schools, were given the opportunity to participate in a large research collaboration without leaving their campuses (Feder, 2005; Howes and others, 2005). Students and their professors were also able to participate in group meetings through videoconferences, where information regarding procedures, results, or problems was discussed (Baumann and others, 2007). The design of the MoNA project allowed for a broad set of students to participate and interact, including graduate, nontraditional, and high school students (Feder, 2005; Baumann and others, 2007).

Of the sixty-two undergraduates who participated in the MoNA program over six years, to date nineteen are in graduate school in physics (five of whom have specifically selected nuclear physics as their area of interest), six are in graduate school in engineering and chemistry, and three are currently high school teachers (Baumann and others, 2007). The MoNA program is a prime example of how research faculty worked together to create an educational experience that not only helped advance the technology of nuclear physics but also helped students and professors from different types of institutions get involved in a research project.

Conditions Conducive to Undergraduate Research and Creative Activities

These exemplary institutional efforts in undergraduate research and creative activities were selected for their well-established history, innovative practices, and breadth of undergraduate research, scholarship, and creative activities. Their faculty, administration, students, and staff work in unison to support and sustain robust undergraduate research programs. These institutions, recognized in the literature on undergraduate research and by many external organizations for their enduring programs, generally share many of the following characteristics:

An established process and program for incorporating students in research;

Longevity—a history of undergraduate research activities;

Support from faculty and administration (human and financial resources);

Efforts to provide outreach and opportunities to diverse student populations (such as underrepresented groups, students of low socioeconomic status, women, and transfer students);

Programs that are part of the institutional budget and mission;

Funding opportunities for faculty and students;

Efforts to celebrate and showcase undergraduates' work;

Continual assessment of undergraduate research programs through faculty, student, and alumni surveys.

It should be noted that many colleges and universities have invested in undergraduate research and share many, if not all, of the above characteristics. For some institutions, undergraduate research and creative activities exist independently in academic units or in honors programs, while other institutions have created centralized offices that provide administrative support to faculty and students involved in research. These case studies provide insight into the evolution, philosophies, and infrastructure of undergraduate research programs.

Studies examining specific characteristics of students who engage in undergraduate research are in short supply. Much of the current literature on undergraduate research and creative activities revolves around reporting how such educational ventures augment student learning (see, for example, Kinkead, 2003; Lanza, 1988; Seago, 1992; Seymour, Hunter, Laursen, and Deantoni, 2004) or provides anecdotal accounts from faculty and students of the effects participation brings about (Campbell and Skoog, 2004; Dotterer, 2002; Kardash, 2000; Siebert, 1988, for example). Some issues such as faculty compensation or limitations on student knowledge and ability tend to be recurring themes in the area of undergraduate research and are fairly well documented (Malachowski, 2003; Voertman, 1970). During a period in which concern for the quality of education is intensifying, many articles have been generated that recount the innovative (or practical) ways in which institutions incorporate inquiry-driven methods or other hands-on experiences across various disciplines (see, for example, Hadley, 1972; Thompson, McNeil, Sherwood, and Stark, 2001; Verity and others, 2002).

Undergraduate research and creative activities have existed at many colleges and universities for some time. Whether they exist in small pockets in academic departments or are campuswide efforts supported (financially and administratively) by a centralized office, many different factors contribute to promoting conditions that foster student engagement in research and creative activities. In an attempt to incorporate research activities in today's undergraduate experience, institutions have formulated various ways of supporting this burgeoning method of teaching and learning. Colleges and universities differ in mission, priorities, faculty, students, institutional culture, and resources and therefore must implement methods most logical for their own needs; note, for example, the wide variety of programs and activities offered at different schools (Kauffman and Stocks, 2003; Merkel, 2003). The following section is a general representation of conditions that aid in the support of undergraduate research.

Financial Resources

Funding is an important aspect of supporting undergraduate research. Although faculty can sometimes hire students through their own grant funding, institutions can also provide experiences to their students through externally supported programs or funds. Some of these programs have specific objectives that provide structure for everything, from participants' characteristics and the activities they participate in to the reporting and accountability requirements for the institution. Other sponsors are more general in nature; that is, funds are intended to support undergraduate research and creative activities and are less focused on students' characteristics.

Some institutions, for example, may be awarded a grant through the NSF to administer a Ronald E. McNair Postbaccalaureate Achievement Program or a Louis Stokes Alliance for Minority Participation Program for underrepresented minorities and to encourage the eventual pursuit of a graduate education. Initiatives that are backed by the NSF provide some resolution to the issue of scarce financial resources to support undergraduate research activities, especially in the STEM fields. Colleges and universities may also secure funding from other agencies that provide a portal to research activities. The Howard Hughes Medical Institute, for example, awards multimillion-dollar grants to institutions through an invitation-only competition for the strengthening of education in biology and biology-related disciplines (Howard Hughes Medical Institute, 2006). The program has several objectives: to integrate research and teaching in undergraduate education; to support students' involvement in faculty research; to prepare undergraduates, including women and members of minority groups underrepresented in the sciences, for graduate studies and for careers in biomedical research, medicine, and science education; and to increase science literacy for all students, including nonscience majors (p. 1).

External sponsorship by corporations or industry is not uncommon in undergraduate research. Amgen (2006), a biotechnology company, provides funding for student stipends in addition to room and board at a participating school and round-trip travel expenses. Similarly, General Motors awards grants for stipends, travel, and equipment to qualified Northwestern University engineering or applied science students (Northwestern University, 2006).

An exploration on any Internet search engine reveals that some schools pull together extensive information on funding opportunities, while others provide limited information. Such collective financial backing from federal and corporate grants provides institutions with additional resources to support research and creative activities for undergraduates.

Private donors serve as another avenue of financial support for undergraduate research programs (Katkin, 2003). In the face of decreasing federal support for higher education, donor support has played an important role in the conception or continuance of many educational initiatives. Some undergraduate research programs are made possible by the contributions of private donors or endowments. Schools such as the University of Michigan–Ann Arbor or MIT have areas on their Web sites designated for giving (or "sponsorship") or prominently feature acknowledgment of donors.

Human Resources

Although many faculty members find working with undergraduates in a collaborative or research setting satisfying, it is often still seen as an additional task that goes unrecognized or as uncompensated work at the cost of one's professional goals and obligations (Russell, 2006; Baenninger and Hakim, 1999; Siebert, 1988; Katkin, 2003; Malachowski, 2003). To receive promotions and tenure, faculty members find that they must protect their time and make prudent choices regarding the activities in which they partake. Because working with undergraduates in a research setting is more demanding in terms of teaching and personal contact, the time and energy devoted to other activities decrease. Unless the institution sets aside funds to support undergraduate research activities, faculty members must choose between backing their graduate students or selecting an undergraduate, who must be trained and closely supervised. Institutional considerations for encouraging and supporting undergraduate research involve assessing and evaluating the use of current resources (human, financial, space) and weighing them against overall institutional goals. If one commits to increased undergraduate research, how will resources be reallocated, and will it come at the cost of other important programs on campus?

Barriers to Undergraduate Research and Creative Activities

Despite the encouraging outcomes associated with undergraduate research and creative activities, some barriers still exist (Carter and others, 1990; Seago, 1992; Siebert, 1988; Kinkead, 2003; Russell, 2006): institutional size, faculty time, equipment and resources, funding, students' interest, the time-consuming nature of training and working with undergraduates, the physical and mental energy required to work with undergraduates, the perception that undergraduates lack appropriate background knowledge and training to conduct meaningful research, and disciplinary cultural barriers in the humanities and social sciences that deter faculty from working with undergraduates on scholarly work.

Rewards associated with research productivity influence the priorities of faculty members, which may also reflect a department's values and norms. Departmental values and norms that emphasize research activities also influence faculty research and teaching preferences (Amey, 1999; Tang and Chamberlain, 1997). Because of faculty research priorities, these environmental and cultural conditions in the institution may therefore indirectly affect students' participation in research activities.

Another issue for undergraduate research activities is the lack of reward and compensation for professors who work with undergraduates on research projects (Boyer Commission on Educating Undergraduates in the Research University, 1998; Kinkead, 2003; Reinvention Center at Stony Brook, 2004). In some situations, professors who choose to supervise undergraduate students are also accepting a teaching overload (often without commensurate compensation), which may discourage some faculty from adding undergraduate research activities to their workloads (Malachowski, 2003). Encouraging faculty members to mentor or supervise more undergraduates in research activities may depend on how interested institutions are able to successfully compensate faculty members in significant ways (Reinvention Center at Stony Brook, 2004).

As previously discussed, theory asserts that the shift away from teaching activities is partly the result of expectations that faculty will undertake research and scholarly work that bring their institutions prominence and prestige. Because current reward structures tend to assign greater weight to research productivity than to teaching in tenure and promotion decisions, faculty members are encouraged to pursue research activities. Faculty reward structures tend to support those who devote more time to research and publication and obtain external funding (Fairweather, 1989). Massy and Zemsky (1994) also point out that quality teaching is not compensated by pay increases or other rewards, while success or failure in research and scholarship carries significant consequences. That is, poor progress in research productivity can mean loss of stature for senior faculty members or tenure and promotion for junior faculty, while poor teaching alone would not result in such loss (Massy and Zemsky, 1994).

Another issue with existing reward structures is the relative ease with which research productivity can be measured in tangible terms such as publications or grants awarded, while effective teaching is more difficult to evaluate because of the variability of practices and philosophies (Tang and Chamberlain, 1997; Boyer Commission on Educating Undergraduates in the Research University, 1998). Russell (2006) found that despite the personal satisfaction that faculty mentors derive from participating in undergraduate research, fewer than four in ten agreed with the statement, "Mentoring undergraduates is viewed favorably in my department's tenure/promotion review process" (p. ES-5). In this regard, the inclusion and recognition of faculty work in undergraduate research as a part of tenure and promotion decisions is a means to encourage more faculty involvement (Malachowski, 2003; Reinvention Center at Stony Brook, 2004). Enhancing faculty reward structures in this way would also demonstrate an institution's recognition and support of the importance of such activities.

Given that participation in undergraduate research activities leads to positive educational outcomes, why is it that such opportunities are not readily available and supported on more college campuses? Several barriers exist that prevent faculty from engaging undergraduates in research and creative opportunities. Chapman (2003) identified two major differences between the nature of undergraduate and graduate education that exacerbate the challenge of involving undergraduates in research activities. First, undergraduate research typically involves replication rather than original study. As such, undergraduate research does not receive the prestige that is attributed to graduate-level research by companies looking for new discoveries. Second, the reward structure is different for conducting research at the undergraduate and graduate levels. Graduate students are able to focus on a particular topic of interest, and the end product is typically a thesis, dissertation, or publication and the establishment of one's name in the field. Undergraduates typically engage in the interests of the faculty member, with the end product being a senior thesis, grade, or presentation.

Faculty members hesitate to engage undergraduates in research and creative activities for a number of reasons. From a faculty member's perspective, involving undergraduates in research is very time-consuming, and time is of the essence for faculty on the tenure track at research universities. According to Zimmer (2005), it takes about two years of working with the same undergraduates for the demands on the faculty member to pay off at a liberal arts college. The ratio may be a little higher at research universities. For undergraduates to engage in a meaningful research experience, they must be properly trained to conduct research. Undergraduate students do not typically take the types of courses needed to fully engage in scientific research; thus, faculty members must spend time teaching the skills necessary to conduct research. Further, such training most often occurs outside the classroom. The practice at most research universities is to hire postdoctoral students and technicians to assist in conducting research, thus leaving undergraduates with fewer opportunities to participate.

From an administrative perspective, barriers to engaging undergraduates in research and creative activities include uncertainty about the overall process, lack of institutional resources, and difficulty identifying skilled researchers to serve as mentors (Ellis, 2006). A number of research institutions may have the desire to provide opportunities for undergraduates to engage in research and creative activities but lack the knowledge necessary to make it happen.

The most successful undergraduate research programs have good support systems in place to keep the program running smoothly. For support programs to provide key services, the institution must provide the research office with adequate resources. Ultimately, an undergraduate research program must have faculty willing to serve as research mentors for undergraduates. And faculty members will be more likely to serve in this capacity if appropriate resources are in place to support programmatic efforts.

Conclusions and Implications

A MERICAN HIGHER EDUCATION is in a critical stage in its development. On the one hand, American higher education remains the envy of the rest of the world for its prominent reputation and for its research productivity. On the other hand, American higher education is constantly criticized for the perceived underachievement in undergraduate education and other issues such as college costs. Undergraduate research and creative activities emerge as a solution to enhance the quality of undergraduate education and to promote students' success in college, as advocated by various groups such as the Council on Undergraduate Research and the Boyer Commission on Educating Undergraduates in the Research University. This section offers some conclusions regarding undergraduate research and creative activities, discusses implications for policy and program development, recommends approaches for program assessment, and indicates directions for additional research regarding undergraduate research and creative activities.

Conclusions

Our thesis points toward the following conclusions about engaging undergraduates in research and creative activities. First, at the theoretical level, undergraduate research and creative activities reflect the principles of how people learn; they also include many features of long-standing educational practices such as experiential learning and "good practices" known in higher education for decades. Second, the empirical evidence suggests participation in undergraduate research and creative activities helps enrich undergraduate students' college experiences and promote student learning outcomes. Not all students, however, have equal access to the benefits associated with such participation. The disparity of participation in undergraduate research and creative activities runs along the familiar lines of gender, race or ethnicity, academic preparation, and disciplinary and institutional characteristics. To continuously improve the quality of undergraduate education, it is desirable not only to further expand opportunities for undergraduate students to participate in such activities but also to narrow the participation gaps for students of different backgrounds and in different environments.

Implications for Policy in Higher Education

Astin (1985a, 1985b, 1993a) has proposed a "talent development" perspective in understanding educational excellence. He also emphasized the importance of maintaining equity in educational opportunity as an integral part of educational excellence. Done properly, undergraduate research and creative activities have the potential to develop the individual talents of students and to promote educational equity, particularly in the STEM fields.

Policymakers at different levels should be keenly interested in promoting students' participation in undergraduate research and creative activities. Concern is growing that the educational enterprise somewhat dampens students' creativity. For instance, Tepper (2006) suggested that many first-year students come to college with genuine curiosity in knowledge discovery but that "most students quickly lose that heightened inquisitiveness. . . . By their senior year, students have been socialized to keep their curiosity in check" (p. 5). Researchers on the development of creativity have suggested that community and environmental factors could play essential roles in addressing these issues. These factors are closely related to what higher educational institutions can offer such as experiences in diversity (both domestic and international), collaboration, and interdisciplinary studies (Harling-Smith, 2006, p. 27). Undergraduate research and creative activities have these essential features. Ellis (2006) argued, "The purpose of such an approach is not for every student to become a scientist or technologist. Rather, it is to create a stronger culture for innovation by immersing all students in intellectually stimulating projects. The scholarship at the core of academic research lays the foundation for innovation: Well-designed research projects intrinsically encourage risk taking as they explore the unknown. Research promotes critical and creative thinking, the habits of mind that nurture innovation; creates a sense of intellectual excitement and adventure; and provides the satisfaction of real accomplishment" (p. B20). As the nation becomes more concerned about maintaining its edge in global competition, the federal government, through its agencies like the NSF, should continue to invest in programs that enhance undergraduate participation in research and creative activities.

Recently, states have played a more active role in higher education. Coupled with the increasing concern about college costs and the affordability of higher education, many states are particularly interested in the performance and accountability of higher education. Undergraduate student learning experiences and outcomes have become constant items in the state agenda. Some argue that "the chance for students to conduct research may well be the best measure available of the quality of an institution's undergraduate education" (Chapman, 2003, p. B5). Not only does it offer a perspective in terms of measuring institutional quality, it is also a strong suggestion that it is in the states' interests to invest in undergraduate research and creative activities to promote students' learning experiences and outcomes.

Initiatives that can promote students' engagement in undergraduate research and creative activities will benefit higher education institutions on multiple fronts. Given that participation can improve student experiences such as improved interaction with the faculty and promote student retention and other educational outcomes, it is indeed at the core interest of higher education institutions as learning organizations. It also contributes to the improvement of institutional prestige and reputation.

The major challenge is finances: providing research and creative activities is not inexpensive. One solution to expand research and creative activity opportunities for students is to link financial aid and student participation in these activities. College costs are a major concern for many students. Each year, the federal government, the states, and higher education institutions pour billions of dollars into student financial aid, some need based and some based on other criteria. Perhaps it would be very beneficial if some of the non-need-based financial aid could be linked with student participation in research and creative activities through the establishment of undergraduate research assistantships. That is, colleges and universities can consider offering financial aid on the basis of student participation in research and creative activities.

Implications for Program Development

The challenge common to all colleges and universities is arranging their resources for learning so that students spend more of their time on the activities that matter to their education. To develop an effective program in undergraduate research and creative activities, it is necessary to consider the two major participants of those activities: the students and the faculty members. Colleges and universities should make an effort to bring research and creative activities to the center of the undergraduate curriculum and to make research experiences, inside or outside the regular curriculum, more widely available to undergraduate students.

Many studies also cite the problem of faculty compensation and recognition as a major challenge in promoting undergraduate research activities. The Boyer Commission on Educating Undergraduates in the Research University (1998) acknowledged that quality teaching is poorly rewarded and claims that the terms "success" and "research productivity" are nearly synonymous at research universities. The commission commented that "the reward structures in the modern research university need to reflect the synergy of teaching and research—and the essential reality of university life: that baccalaureate students are the university's life blood and are increasingly self-aware" (p. 32).

Colleges and universities need to develop and implement effective programs in undergraduate research and creative activities and to avoid the pitfalls. First, it is desirable to institute an organizational structure that is conducive to the enhancement of undergraduate engagement in research and creative activities. Second, even more important, it is imperative to foster a culture among both students and faculty members that values undergraduate participation in research and creative activities.

It is important to recognize that despite the beneficial outcomes associated with research experiences, such activities are not appropriate for all students, nor do all students wish to become involved in research work. Therefore, when an institution does institute programs for undergraduate research and creative activities, it might be more productive to allow students to participate voluntarily, with strong encouragement and hortatory policy (such as slogans and signs), rather than a requirement that students participate in such programs.

Approaches to Assessing Programs for Undergraduate Research and Creative Activities

To provide evidence of the effects of undergraduate research and creative activity or to continuously improve the effectiveness of such programs, periodic assessment of those programs is necessary. First and foremost, however, those who are involved in such programs or whoever is concerned about the effectiveness of such programs need to clarify the objectives of the program. This step is critical, because the program is likely to produce a wide range of outcomes that could affect the students, the faculty, and the institution as a whole.

According to Astin's I-E-O model, educational outcomes can be related to both the input and environment. The I-E-O model is more of a conceptual perspective in understanding how environment may affect the outcomes. Even though it is more widely used with the quantitative method, the model itself can be used either using a quantitative or a qualitative approach. When the interest is on the effectiveness of a program in undergraduate research and creative activity, such a program should be considered as a part of the environment.

To assess the programs in undergraduate research and creative activities, two major types of assessment activities can be undertaken. The first type is to assess the environment—the program itself—either through interviews or surveys of the participants to identify the components and features of the program that participants are satisfied with. The second type of assessment focuses on the effectiveness of the program on desirable outcomes, determined by the program's objectives. The assessment of effectiveness examines whether and to what extent the program makes a difference in the participants with respect to outcomes. This type of assessment is usually undertaken from a quantitative perspective in a multistep approach (Terenzini and Upcraft, 1996).

First, the assessment team needs to determine the population and the strategy by drawing a sample that is a good representation of the population to be studied. Second, following Astin's I-E-O model, the team must identify the input variables related to the outcome variables so that they can be controlled. Third, environment variables must be determined and differentiated between those variables of interest (such as program participation) and other environmental variables. It is appropriate to conceptualize "program participation" as the dependent variable and other environmental variables as control variables; at this point, it is also important to consider what modes of statistical analysis will be used.

After the variables are identified, it is critical to select or develop instruments to measure all relevant variables and to effectively collect data from the sample. The next step is to convert the raw data into a usable format and to conduct appropriate data analysis. Finally, it is important to report the assessment results in appropriate formats so that constituents and decision makers can understand them. This step is important because it can directly influence the program and the possible strategies for using the assessment results.

Additional Research Needed

Engaging undergraduate students in research and creative activities has come to center stage in the arena of undergraduate education reform. It shows great promise from the standpoint of conceptual evidence. The accompanying empirical evidence is starting to accumulate as more research and evaluative studies emerge and have confirmed the positive impacts on students. Additional research on the impacts of participation in undergraduate research and creative activities, however, would help policymakers and higher education administrators make more informed decisions.

First, given that the world has essentially become a global village and that competition from outside the United States has intensified, demands are increasing on colleges and universities to help maintain an American advantage in the age of globalization. Educating students with creativity and innovative spirit has been advocated as one way of achieving that goal (Ellis, 2006). Even though it is argued that students' participation in undergraduate research and creative activities may help, empirical evidence to support the argument is absent. Greater efforts to examining the relationship between participation in undergraduate research and creative activities and the development of student creativity and innovative spirit would shed new light on the effects of engagement in research and creative activities.

Second, because existing undergraduate research and creative activities vary widely, it would be useful to understand how and why different features of those programs affect students. Further, the distillation of conditions that might moderate the effects of those programs on student outcomes would be useful. For example, are there differences in gains for students who do independent research such as an individual capstone project compared with those who work collaboratively with a faculty member on a project? Does it matter how much time (per week, per summer, per semester, per year) students spend and the specific nature of their contributions (design the study, collect data, analyze findings, report results)? Does it make a difference as to whether the student is compensated for participating or where the research is done (library, laboratory, in the field)? Answers to these questions would help us better understand how to use undergraduate research more effectively to enhance students' learning and personal development.

Finally, improved inquiry methods necessary for research and assessment of undergraduate research activities would help provide more convincing evidence. A common shortcoming in the existing research literature is consideration of the potential differences for students who choose to participate in undergraduate research and those who do not, because participation is not a random event. Future research should consider strategies to deal with this type of selection bias in examining the effects of participation in undergraduate research and creative activities.

As this monograph has demonstrated, undergraduate engagement in research and creative activities can by and large benefit students, faculty mentors, colleges and universities, and the knowledge industry. This assertion has been consistently confirmed by empirical studies in different disciplines through qualitative, quantitative, and mixed-method approaches. As assessment techniques of student learning and developmental outcomes improve and more advanced analytical methods are used to evaluate program effects on constituents, a more comprehensive understanding can be developed. This important next step will further provide stronger evidence to decide the next step in undergraduate education reform for colleges and universities and for all groups concerned about the quality of higher education.

Appendix: Resources for Undergraduate Research and Creative Activities

Opportunities for Students

Abbott Laboratories Internship Program: http://www.abbott.com/global/url/ content/en_US/50.60.10:10/general_content/General_Content_00166.htm

American Psychological Society Undergraduate Research Fellowship: http://www.the-aps.org/education/undergrad/stuaward.html

Howard Hughes Medical Institute: http://www.hhmi.org/grants/

NASA Undergraduate Student Research Program: http://www.nasa.gov/audience/ forstudents/postsecondary/learning/Undergraduate_Student_Research_ Program.html

National Science Foundation (NSF/REU): http://www.nsf.gov/funding/pgm_ summ.jsp?pims_id=5517andfrom=fund

Ronald E. McNair Postbaccalaureate Achievement Program: http://www.ed. gov/programs/triomcnair/index.html

Summer Undergraduate Research Fellowship, National Institute of Standards and Technology: http://www.surf.nist.gov/surf2.htm

Tahoe-Baikal Institute: http://www.tahoebaikal.org/projects/exchange

U.S. Department of Energy, Office of Science: http://www.scied.science. doe.gov/scied/sci_ed.htm

Organizations and Conferences

American Chemical Society: http://www.chemistry.org/portal/a/c/s/1/acsdisplay. html?DOC=education<\\>student<\\>studaffs.html

American Physical Society Conference Experience for Undergraduates: http://physics.westmont.edu/ceu/

Atlantic Coast Conference Meeting of the Minds Conference: (sponsored by the ACC International Academic Collaboration, http://www.acciac.org/)

Council on Undergraduate Research: http://www.cur.org/

National Conferences for Undergraduate Research: http://www.ncur.org/

Project Kaleidoscope: http://www.pkal.org/

Sigma Xi Student Research Conference: http://www.sigmaxi.org/meetings/annual/index.shtml

Web Guide to Research for Undergraduates (WebGURU): http://www.webguru.neu.edu/

Selected Undergraduate Research Journals

Journal of Undergraduate Research, Department of Energy: http://www.scied.science.doe.gov/scied/JUR.html

Journal of Young Investigators: http://www.jyi.org/

Sunoikisis Undergraduate Research Symposium in Classics (sponsored by the National Institute for Technology and Liberal Education/NITLE): http://sunoikisis.nitle.org/undergradsymposium/

Undergraduate Research Journals: http://www.cur.org/ugjournal.html

References

Amey, M. J. (1999). *Faculty culture and college life: Reshaping incentives toward student out-comes.* New Directions for Higher Education, no. 105. San Francisco: Jossey-Bass.

Amgen. (2006). *Amgen Scholars Program.* Retrieved March 31, 2007, from http://www.amgenscholars.com/.

Association of American Colleges and Universities. (2002a). *Greater expectations: A new vision for learning as a nation goes to college.* Washington, DC: Association of American Colleges and Universities.

Association of American Colleges and Universities. (2002b). *The student as scholar: Undergradu-ate research and creative practice.* Washington, DC: Association of American Colleges and Universities. Retrieved June 30, 2006, from http://www.aacu.org/meetings/undergraduate_research/index.cfm.

Association of American Colleges and Universities. (2007). *College learning for the new global century.* Washington, DC: Association of American Colleges and Universities.

Astin, A. W. (1977). *Four critical years.* San Francisco: Jossey-Bass.

Astin, A. W. (1985a). *Achieving educational excellence: A critical assessment of priorities and practices in higher education.* San Francisco: Jossey-Bass.

Astin, A. W. (1985b). Involvement: The cornerstone of excellence. *Change, 17,* 35–39.

Astin, A. W. (1993a). *Assessment for excellence: The philosophy and practice of assessment and evaluation in higher education.* Phoenix, AZ: American Council on Education and Oryx Press.

Astin, A. W. (1993b). *What matters in college? Four critical years revisited.* San Francisco: Jossey-Bass.

Baenninger, M., and Hakim, T. (1999, September). Undergraduate research as a curricular element: Multidisciplinary courses at The College of New Jersey. *Council on Undergradu-ate Research Quarterly,* 8–13.

Baird, L. L. (1974). The practical utility of measures of college environments. *Review of Edu-cational Research, 44,* 307–329.

Baird, L. L. (2005). College environments and climates: Assessments and their theoretical assumptions. In J. C. Smart (Ed.), *Higher education: Handbook of theory and research* (Vol. 20, pp. 507–538). New York: Agathon.

Barell, J. (2006). *Problem-based learning: An inquiry approach* (2nd ed.). Thousand Oaks, CA: Corwin Press.

Barrows, H. S., and Tamblyn, R. M. (1980). *Problem-based learning: An approach to medical education.* New York: Springer.

Bauer, K. W. (2001, June). *The effect of participation in undergraduate research on critical thinking and reflective judgement.* Paper presented at the annual forum of the Association for Institutional Research, Long Beach, CA.

Bauer, K. W., and Bennett, J. S. (2003). Alumni perceptions used to assess undergraduate research experience. *Journal of Higher Education, 74,* 210–230.

Baumann, T., and others. (2007). *MoNA white paper: Status report and future plans.* Retrieved January 25, 2007, from http://www.cord.edu/dept/physics/mona/.

Bean, J. P., and Kuh, G. D. (1984). The relationship between student-faculty interaction and undergraduate grade point average. *Research in Higher Education, 21,* 461–477.

Bloom, B. S. (1956). *Taxonomy of educational objectives.* Handbook 1: *The cognitive domain.* New York: McKay.

Bok, D. C. (2006). *Our underachieving colleges: A candid look at how much students learn and why they should be learning more.* Princeton, NJ: Princeton University Press.

Boyer Commission on Educating Undergraduates in the Research University. (1998). *Reinventing undergraduate education: A blueprint for America's research universities.* Stony Brook, NY: Carnegie Foundation for the Advancement of Teaching.

Boyer Commission on Educating Undergraduates in the Research University. (2003). *Reinventing undergraduate education: Three years after the Boyer Report.* Stony Brook, NY: Carnegie Foundation for the Advancement of Teaching.

Braxton, J. M., Eimers, M. T., and Bayer, A. E. (1996). The implications of teaching norms for the improvement of undergraduate education. *Journal of Higher Education, 67,* 603–625.

Brubacher, J. S. (1982). *On the philosophy of higher education.* San Francisco: Jossey-Bass.

Bruner, J. (1966). *Toward a theory of instruction.* Cambridge, MA: Harvard University Press.

Bruner, J. (1985). Vygotsky: Historical and conceptual perspective. In J. V. Wertsch (Ed.), *Culture, communication, and cognition: Vygotskian perspectives* (pp. 21–35). Cambridge: Cambridge University Press.

Campbell, A., and Skoog, G. (2004). Preparing undergraduate women for science careers: Facilitating success in professional research. *Journal of College Science Teaching, 33,* 24–26.

Campbell, A. M. (2002). "The influences and factors of an undergraduate research program in preparing women for science careers." Unpublished doctoral dissertation, Texas Tech University.

Carter, J. L., and others. (1990). The state of the biology major. *Bioscience, 40,* 678–683.

Cech, T. R. (2003). Rebalancing teaching and research. *Science, 299,* 165.

Chapman, D. W. (2003, September 12). Undergraduate research: Showcasing young scholars. *Chronicle of Higher Education,* p. B5.

Chickering, A. W., and Gamson, Z. F. (1987). Seven principles for good practice in undergraduate education. *American Association of Higher Education Bulletin, 39,* 3–7.

Chickering, A. W., and Gamson, Z. F. (1991). *Applying the Seven Principles for Good Practice in Undergraduate Education.* New Directions for Teaching and Learning, No. 47, San Francisco: Jossey-Bass.

Chopin, S. F. (2002). Undergraduate research experiences: The translation of science education from reading to doing. *Anatomical Record (New Anatomist), 269,* 3–10.

Clark, B. R. (1995). *Places of inquiry: Research and advanced education in modern universities.* Berkeley: University of California Press.

Clark, B. R. (1997). The modern integration of research activities with teaching and learning. *Journal of Higher Education, 68,* 241–255.

Council on Undergraduate Research. (2003). *Faculty-undergraduate collaborative research and publishing.* Retrieved September 5, 2005, from http://www.cur.org/wp_respub.html.

Council on Undergraduate Research and National Conference for Undergraduate Research. (2005). *Joint statement of principles in support of undergraduate research, scholarship, and creative activities.* Retrieved June 30, 2006, from http://www.cur.org/SummitPosition.html.

Dewey, J. (1997). *Experience and education.* New York: Simon & Schuster.

Dotterer, R. L. (2002). Student-faculty collaborations, undergraduate research, and collaboration as an administrative model. In K. Zahorski (Ed.), *New Directions for Teaching and Learning* (pp. 81–89). San Francisco: Jossey-Bass.

Driscoll, M. P. (1993). *Psychology of learning for instruction.* Boston: Allyn & Bacon.

Eddins, W., and others. (1997). Searching for a prominent role of research in undergraduate education: Project Interface. *Journal on Excellence in College Teaching, 8,* 69–81.

Education Commission of the States. (1995). *Making quality count in undergraduate education.* Denver: Education Commission of the States.

Elgren, T., and Hensel, N. (2006). Undergraduate research experiences: Synergies between scholarship and teaching. *Peer Review, 8*(1), 4–7.

Ellis, A. B. (2006, April 14). Creating a culture for innovation. *Chronicle of Higher Education, 52*(32), B20.

Eyler, J., and Giles, D. E. (1999). *Where's the learning in service-learning?* San Francisco: Jossey-Bass.

Fairweather, J. S. (1989). Academic research and instruction: The industrial connection. *Journal of Higher Education, 60,* 388–407.

Feder, T. (2005). Undergraduates assemble neutron detector. *Physics Today, 58*(3). Retrieved February 2, 2007, from http://ptonline.aip.org/dbt/dbt.jsp?KEY=PHTOAD&Volume=58&Issue=3.

Florida State University. (2007). *Undergraduate research program in the humanities.* Tallahassee: Florida State University.

Geiger, R. (2004). *Knowledge and money: Research universities and the paradox of the marketplace.* Stanford, CA: Stanford University Press.

Graff, G. (2006). *On defining "research."* Retrieved June 30, 2006, from http://www.reinventioncenter.miami.edu/Spotlights/.

Greendyke, R. B. (2002, November). *Graduate level research from undergraduate students: The lessons learned by student and professor alike.* Paper presented at the 32nd ASEE/IEEE Frontiers in Education Conference, Boston, MA.

Gregerman, S. (1999, December). Improving academic success of diverse students through undergraduate research. *Council on Undergraduate Research Quarterly,* 54–59.

Grinnell College. (2007). *MAP program.* Retrieved August 16, 2007, from http://www.grinnell.edu/offices/dean/MAP/.

Hadley, C. D. (1972). Teaching political scientists: The centrality of research. *PS, 5,* 262–270.

Hakim, T. (1998). Soft assessment of undergraduate research: Reactions and student perspectives. *Council on Undergraduate Research Quarterly,* 189–192.

Harling-Smith, T. (2006). Creativity research review: Some lessons for higher education. *Peer Review, 8*(2), 23–27.

Harvey Mudd College. (2007). *Research.* Retrieved August 20, 2007, from http://www.hmc.edu/academicsclinicresearch/research1.html.

Hathaway, R. S., Nagda, B. A., and Gregerman, S. R. (2002). The relationship of undergraduate research participation to graduate and professional education pursuit: An empirical study. *Journal of College Student Development, 43,* 614–631.

Hmelo-Silver, C. E. (2004). Problem-based learning: What and how do students learn? *Educational Psychology Review, 16,* 235–266.

Hoopes, M. (1993). For undergraduates, hands-on research and book learning go hand in hand. *Scientist, 7*(4), 10.

Howard Hughes Medical Institute. (2006). *Howard Hughes Medical Institute.* Retrieved April 23, 2007, from http://www.hhmi.org/.

Howes, R. H., and others. (2005). Fabrication of a modular array: A collaborative approach to undergraduate research. *American Journal of Physics, 73*(2), 122–126.

Hu, S. (2005). *Beyond grade inflation: grading problems in higher education.* San Francisco: Jossey-Bass.

Hu, S., & Kuh, G. D. (2003). Maximizing what students get out of college: Testing a learning productivity model. *Journal of College Student Development, 44,* 185–203.

Hu, S., Kuh, G. D., and Gayles, J. G. (2007). Engaging undergraduate students in research activities: Are research universities doing a better job? *Innovative Higher Education, 32,* 167–177.

Hu, S., Kuh, G. D., and Li, S. (2007, November). *The effects of inquiry-oriented activities on student learning and personal development.* Paper presented at the annual meeting of the Association for the Study of Higher Education (ASHE), Louisville, KY.

Ishiyama, J. (2002). Does early participation in undergraduate research benefit social science and humanities students? *College Student Journal, 36,* 380–386.

James, P. (1998). Progressive development of deep learning skills through undergraduate and postgraduate dissertations. *Educational Studies, 24,* 95–105.

Jonides, J., von Hippel, W., Lerner, J. S., and Nagda, B. A. (1992, August). *Evaluation of minority retention programs: The Undergraduate Research Opportunities Program at the*

University of Michigan. Paper presented at the annual meeting of the American
Psychological Association, Washington, DC.

Kardash, C. M. (2000). Evaluation of an undergraduate research experience: Perceptions of
undergraduate interns and their faculty mentors. *Journal of Educational Psychology, 92,*
191–201.

Karukstis, K. K., and Elgren, T. E. (Eds.). (2007). *Developing and sustaining a research-supportive
curriculum.* Washington, DC: Council on Undergraduate Research.

Katkin, W. (2003). The Boyer Commission report and its impact on undergraduate research. In
J. Kinkead (Ed.), *Valuing and supporting undergraduate research* (pp. 19–38). San Francisco:
Jossey-Bass.

Kauffman, L. R., and Stocks, J. (Eds.). (2003). *Reinvigorating the undergraduate experience:
Successful models supported by NSF's AIRE/RAIRE program.* Washington, DC: Council on
Undergraduate Research.

Kellogg Commission on the Future of State and Land-Grant Universities. (1997). *Returning
to our roots: The student experience.* Washington, DC: National Association of State
Universities and Land-Grant Colleges.

Kinkead, J. (Ed.). (2003). *Valuing and supporting undergraduate research.* New Directions for
Teaching and Learning, no. 93. San Francisco: Jossey-Bass.

Kolb, D. (1984). *Experiential learning: Experiences as the source of learning and development.*
Englewood Cliffs, NJ: Prentice Hall.

Krathwohl, D. R. (1998). *Methods of educational and social science research: An integrated
approach.* New York: Longman.

Krathwohl, D. R., Bloom, B. S., and Bertram, B. M. (1973). *Taxonomy of educational objectives: The classification of educational goals.* Handbook 2: *Affective domain.* New York:
McKay.

Kremer, J. F., and Bringle, R. G. (1990). The effects of an intensive research experience on
the careers of talented undergraduates. *Journal of Research and Development in Education,
24,* 1–5.

Kuh, G. D., and Hu, S. (2001). Learning productivity at research universities. *Journal of
Higher Education, 72,* 1–28.

Kuh, G. D., Kinzie, J., Buckley, J. A., Bridges, B. K., Hayek, J. C. (2007). Piecing Together
the Student Success Puzzle: Research, Propositions, and Recommendations. ASHE
Higher Education Report, Volume 32, Number 5. San Francisco: Jossey-Bass.

Kuh, G. D., Kinzie, J., Schuh, J. H., and Whitt, E. J. (2005). *Student success in college: Creating
conditions that matter.* San Francisco: Jossey-Bass.

Lanza, J. (1988). Whys and hows of undergraduate research. *Bioscience, 38,* 110–112.

Lanza, J., and Smith, G. C. (1988). Undergraduate research: A little experience goes a long
way. *Journal of College Science Teaching, 18,* 118–120.

Light, R. J. (2001). *Making the most of college: Students speak their minds.* Cambridge, MA:
Harvard University Press.

Loo, C. M., and Rolison, G. (1986). Alienation of ethnic minority students at a predominantly white university. *Journal of Higher Education, 57,* 58–77.

Lopatto, D. (2004). Survey of undergraduate research experience (SURE): First findings. *Cell Biology Education, 3,* 270–277.

Lucas, C. J. (1996). *American higher education: A history.* New York: Palgrave Macmillan.

Madrazo-Peterson, R., and Rodriguez, M. (1978). Minority students' perceptions of a university environment. *Journal of College Student Personnel, 19,* 259–263.

Malachowski, M. R. (2003). A research-across-the-curriculum movement. In J. Kinkead (Ed.), *Valuing and supporting undergraduate research* (pp. 55–68). San Francisco: Jossey-Bass.

Massy, W. F., and Zemsky, R. (1994). Faculty discretionary time: Departments and the "academic ratchet." *Journal of Higher Education, 65,* 1–22.

McDorman, T. (2004). Promoting undergraduate research in the humanities: Three collaborative approaches. *CUR Quarterly, 25,* 39–42.

McKinney, K., Saxe, D., and Cobb, L. (1998). Are we really doing all we can for our undergraduates? Professional socialization via out-of-class experiences. *Teaching Sociology, 26,* 1–13.

Merkel, C. A. (2001). *Undergraduate research at six research universities: A pilot study for the Association of American Universities.* Pasadena: California Institute of Technology.

Merkel, C. A. (2003). Undergraduate research at the research universities. In J. Kinkead (Ed.), *Valuing and supporting undergraduate research* (pp. 39–53). San Francisco: Jossey-Bass.

Mervis, J. (2001). Student research: What is it good for? *Science, 293,* 1614–1615.

Metzger, W. (1955). *Academic freedom in the age of the university.* New York: Columbia University Press.

Nagda, B. A., and others. (1998). Undergraduate student-faculty research partnerships affect student retention. *Review of Higher Education, 22,* 55–72.

National Commission on the Future of Higher Education. (2006). *A test of leadership: Charting the future of U.S. higher education.* Washington, DC: U.S. Department of Education.

National Survey of Student Engagement. (2003). *Converting data into action: Expanding the boundaries of institutional improvement.* Bloomington: Center for Postsecondary Research, Indiana University.

National Survey of Student Engagement. (2004). *Student engagement: Pathways to collegiate success.* Bloomington: Center for Postsecondary Research, Indiana University.

National Survey of Student Engagement. (2005). *Student engagement: Exploring different dimensions of student engagement.* Bloomington: Center for Postsecondary Research, Indiana University.

Nnadozie, E., Ishiyama, J., and Chon, J. (2001). Undergraduate research internships and graduate school success. *Journal of College Student Development, 42,* 145–156.

Northwestern University. (2006). *GM/EXCEL undergraduate research grant.* Retrieved April 23, 2007, from http://www.mccormick.northwestern.edu/undergraduate/index.php.

Paalman, M. H. (2002). Undergraduate research, education, and the future of science. *Anatomical Record (New Anatomist), 269,* 1–2.

Pace, R. C. (1979). *Measuring outcomes of college.* San Francisco: Jossey-Bass.

Pascarella, E. T. (1985). College environmental influences on learning and cognitive development: A critical review and synthesis. In J. C. Smart (Ed.), *Higher education: Handbook of theory and research.* Vol. 1 (pp. 1–62). New York: Agathon.

Pascarella, E. T., and Terenzini, P. T. (1979). Student-faculty informal contact and college persistence: A further investigation. *Journal of Educational Research, 72,* 214–218.

Pascarella, E. T., and Terenzini, P. T. (1991). *How college affects students: Findings and insights from twenty years of research.* San Francisco: Jossey-Bass.

Pascarella, E. T., and Terenzini, P. T. (2005). *How college affects students: A third decade of research* (2nd ed.). San Francisco: Jossey-Bass.

Paul, E. L. (2006). Community-based research as scientific and civic pedagogy. *Peer Review: Emerging Trends and Key Debates in Undergraduate Education, 8,* 12–15.

Peppas, N. A. (1981, Summer). Student preparations for graduate school through undergraduate research. *Chemical Engineering Education, 15,* 135–137.

Perez, J. A. (2003). Undergraduate research at two-year colleges. In J. Kinkead (Ed.), *Valuing and supporting undergraduate research* (pp. 69–77). San Francisco: Jossey-Bass.

Powell, K., and Stiller, J. (2005). What's living in your world? Building research partnerships for inquiry-based learning. *Science Teacher, 72,* 20–25.

Reinvention Center at Stony Brook. (2004). *Integrating research into undergraduate education: The value added.* Stony Brook, NY: Reinvention Center at Stony Brook.

Rogers, V. D. (2003). Surviving the "culture shock" of undergraduate research in the humanities. *CUR Quarterly, 23,* 132–135.

Rudolph, F. (1977). *Curriculum: A history of the American undergraduate course of study since 1636.* Carnegie Council Series on Policy Studies in Higher Education. San Francisco: Jossey-Bass.

Rudolph, F. (1990). *American College and University: A history.* Athens, GA: University of Georgia Press.

Russell, S. H. (2006). *Evaluation of NSF support for undergraduate research opportunities: Draft synthesis report.* (SRI Project P16346). Menlo Park, CA: SRI International.

Sakalys, J. A. (1984). Effects of an undergraduate research course on cognitive development. *Nursing Research, 33,* 290–295.

Seago, J. L. (1992). The role of research in undergraduate instruction. *American Biology Teacher, 54,* 401–405.

Seaman, B. (2005). *Binge: Campus life in an age of disconnection and excess.* Hoboken, NJ: Wiley.

Seymour, E., Hunter, A., Laursen, S. L., and Deantoni, T. (2004). Establishing the benefits of research experiences for undergraduates in the sciences: First findings from a three-year study. *Science Education, 88,* 493–534.

Siebert, E. D. (1988). Undergraduate research: Is it really worth it? *Journal of College Science Teaching, 18,* 92–97.

Slavin, R. E. (2002). Evidence-based education policies: Transforming educational practice and research. *Educational Researcher, 31*(7), 15–21.

Strange, C. C. (2003). Dynamics of campus environments. In S.R. Komives, D. B. Woodard, and Associates (Eds.), *Student services: A handbook for the profession* (4th ed.). San Francisco: Jossey-Bass.

Strassburger, J. (1995). Embracing undergraduate research. *AAHE Bulletin, 47,* 3–5.

Swager, S. L. (1997). *Faculty/student interaction in an undergraduate research program: Task and interpersonal elements.* Unpublished doctoral dissertation, University of Michigan.

Tang, T. L., and Chamberlain, M. (1997). Attitudes toward research and teaching: Differences between administrators and faculty members. *Journal of Higher Education, 68,* 212–227.

Tepper, S. T. (2006). Taking the measure of the creative campus. *Peer Review, 8*(2), 4–7.

Terenzini, P. T., and Upcraft, M. L. (1996). Using quantitative methods. In M. L. Upcraft and J. Schuh (Eds.), *Assessment in student affairs* (pp. 84–112). San Francisco: Jossey-Bass.

Thompson, C. J., McNeil, J. A., Sherwood, G. D., and Stark, P. L. (2001). Using collaborative research to facilitate student learning. *Western Journal of Nursing Research, 23,* 504–516.

Tinto, V. (1975). Dropout from higher education: A theoretical synthesis of recent research. *Review of Educational Research, 45,* 89–125.

Tinto, V. (1993). *Leaving college: Rethinking the causes and cures of student attrition.* Chicago: University of Chicago Press.

Tompkins, L. (1998). Being a scientist: One woman's experience. In A. Pattatucci (Ed.), *Women in science: Meeting career challenges* (pp. 110–115). Thousand Oaks, CA: Sage.

Trow, M. (1974). Problems in the transition from elite to mass higher education. In *Policies for higher education* (pp. 51–101). Paris: OECD.

University of Central Florida. (2007). *UCF undergraduate research opportunities.* Retrieved April 23, 2007, from http://www.undergrad.ucf.edu/researchchart/.

Verity, P. G., and others. (2002). Improving undergraduate research experiences: Lessons learned from a historically black university's unusual collaboration. *AAHE Bulletin, 54*(6), 3–6.

Veysey, L. (1965). *The emergence of the American university.* Chicago: University of Chicago Press.

Voertman, R. F. (1970). Undergraduate research aid to educational relevance. *Educational Record, 51,* 72–80.

Volkwein, J. F., and Carbone, D. A. (1994). The impact of departmental research and teaching climates on undergraduate growth and satisfaction. *Journal of Higher Education, 65,* 147–167.

Vygotsky, L. S. (1978). Mind in society: The development of higher psychological processes. M. Cole, V. John-Steiner, S. Scribner, and E. Souberma (Eds.). Cambridge, MA: Harvard University Press.

Wasserman, E. R. (2000). *The door in the dream: Conversations with eminent women in science.* Washington, DC: Joseph Henry Press.

Weidman, J. C. (1979). Nonintellective undergraduate socialization in academic departments. *Journal of Higher Education, 50,* 48–62.

Weidman, J. C. (1989). Undergraduate socialization: A conceptual approach. In J. C. Smart (Ed.), *Higher education: Handbook of theory and research* (Vol. 5, pp. 289–322). New York: Agathon.

Werner, T. C., and Sorum, C. E. (2003). From engineering to English: Encouraging undergraduate research across the disciplines. In L. R. Kauffman and J. E. Stocks (Eds.), *Reinvigorating the undergraduate experience: Successful models supported by NSF's AIRE/RAIRE program.* Retrieved June 30, 2006, from http://www.cur.org/publications/aire_raire/toc.asp.

Wertsch, J. V. (1984). The zone of proximal development: Some conceptual issues. In B. Rogoff and J. V. Wertsch (Eds.), *Children's learning in the zone of proximal development* (pp. 7–18). San Francisco: Jossey-Bass.

Wingspread Group on Higher Education. (1993). *An American imperative: Higher expectations for higher education.* Racine, WI: Johnson Foundation.

Wray, D. D. (2000). *The effectiveness of undergraduate researchers and the effect of undergraduate research on the student.* Unpublished doctoral dissertation, Idaho State University.

Wubah, D., and others. (2000). Retention of minority students through research. *Council on Undergraduate Research Quarterly, 20,* 120–126.

Yavneh, N., and Ersing, R. (2007). *Expanding the scope of the REU: Innovative Approaches at USF.* Retrieved August 20, 2007, from http://www.reinventioncenter.miami.edu/Spotlights/#sflorida.

Zimmer, M. (2005, August 12). How to find students' inner geek. *Chronicle of Higher Education*, B5.

Name Index

A
Amey, M. J., 71
Astin, A. W., 25, 27, 28, 33, 34, 53, 76

B
Baenninger, M., 70
Baird, L. L., 26
Barrell, J., 22
Barrows, H. S., 22
Bauer, K. W., 35, 36, 37, 51, 53
Baumann, T., 66
Bayer, A. E., 53
Bean, J. P., 34
Bennett, J. S., 35, 36, 37, 51, 53
Bertram, B. M., 27, 33
Bloom, B. S., 27, 33
Bok, D. C., 1
Braxton, J. M., 53
Bringle, R. G., 5, 6, 8, 9, 10
Brubacher, J. S., 5
Bruner, J., 19, 20

C
Campbell, A. M., 37, 68
Carbone, D. A., 36, 53, 54
Carter, J. L., 71
Cech, T. R., 41, 42
Chamberlain, M., 71, 72
Chapman, D. W., 72, 77
Chickering, A. W., 28, 29
Chon, J., 35, 38, 40

Chopin, S. F., 41, 42
Cobb, L., 8, 29, 30, 53

D
Deantoni, T., 5, 6, 23, 34, 37, 52, 53, 68
Dewey, J., 21
Dotterer, R. L., 68
Driscoll, M. P., 19

E
Eddins, W., 36
Eimers, M. T., 53
Elgren, T. E., 2, 6, 43, 58
Ellis, A. B., 73, 74, 76
Ersing, R., 63
Eyler, J., 23, 24

F
Fairweather, J. S., 72
Feder, T., 66

G
Gamson, Z., 28, 29
Gayles, J. G., 2, 45, 46, 50, 54, 58
Geiger, R., 5
Giles, D. E., 23, 24
Graff, G., 7
Greendyke, R. B., 41
Gregerman, S., 35
Gregerman, S. R., 39

H

Hadley, C. D., 68
Hakim, T., 7, 40, 57, 70
Harling-Smith, T., 76
Hathaway, R. S., 39
Hensel, N., 6, 43
Hmelo-Silver, C. E., 22
Hoopes, M., 42
Howes, R. H., 41, 65, 66
Hu, S., 2, 26, 38, 45, 46, 50, 54, 58
Humboldt**, 14, 15
Hunter, A., 5, 6, 23, 34, 37, 52, 53, 68

I

Ishiyama, J., 8, 9, 10, 35, 36, 38, 40

J

James, P., 36
Jonides, J., 353

K

Kardash, C. M., 51, 68
Karukstis, K. K., 2, 58
Katkin, W., 47, 58, 70
Kauffman, L. R., 68
Kinkead, J., 5, 6, 10, 39, 68, 71
Kinzie, J., 28, 29, 34, 65
Kolb, D., 21
Krathwohl, D. R., 3, 27, 33
Kremer, J. F., 5, 6, 8, 9, 10
Kuh, G. D., 2, 26, 28, 29, 34, 38, 45, 46, 50, 54, 58, 65

L

Lanza, J., 6, 53, 68
Laursen, S. L., 5, 6, 23, 34, 37, 52, 53, 68
Lerner, J. S., 35
Li, S., 38
Light, R. J., 34
Loo, C. M., 38
Lopatto, D., 36, 37, 42
Lucas, C. J., 5

M

McDorman, T., 10, 11, 12
McKinney, K., 8, 29, 30, 53

McNeil, J. A., 5, 68
Madrazo-Peterson, R., 38
Malachowski, M. R., 68, 70, 71, 72
Massy, W. F., 72
Merkel, C. A., 16, 68
Mervis, J., 41, 42

N

Nagda, B. A., 35, 38, 39
Nnadozie, E., 35, 38, 40

P

Paalman, M. H., 41
Pace, R. C., 28
Pascarella, E. T., 26, 28, 31, 33, 34, 53, 58
Paul, E. L., 23
Peppas, N. A., 8, 36
Perez, J. A., 65
Powell, K., 9

R

Rodgriquez, M., 38
Rogers, V. D., 12
Rolison, G., 38
Rudolph, F., 13, 14
Russell, S. H., 6, 37, 39, 42, 50, 51, 52, 54, 70, 71, 72

S

Sakalya, J. A., 36
Saxe, D., 8, 29, 30, 53
Schuh, J. H., 28, 29, 34, 65
Seago, J. L., 5, 23, 68, 71
Seaman, B., 34
Seymour, E., 5, 6, 23, 34, 37, 42, 52, 53, 68
Sherwood, G. D., 5, 8, 68
Siebert, E. D., 5, 51, 68, 70, 71
Skoog, G., 68
Smith, G. C., 6, 53
Sorum, C. E., 11
Stark, P. L., 5, 8, 68
Stiller, J., 9
Stocks, J., 68
Strange, C. C., 26
Strassburger, J., 6, 23, 51
Swager, S. L., 35

Subject Index

A

Academic achievement, 36

Academic integration, 31–32

Accountability issue, 2

American Association of Colleges and Universities (AAC&U), 4

American Chemical Society, 65

Amgen, 69

Association of American Colleges and Universities, 1, 2, 5

B

"Beacon Associate Colleges," 65

Boyer Commission on Educating Undergraduates in the Research University (1998), 1, 2, 39, 47, 71, 72, 75, 78

Bridge Summer Research Program (UCLA), 39

C

California Institute of Technology, 16

Career selection, 37–38

Carnegie Academy for the Scholarship of Teaching and Learning (CASTL), 64

Center for Undergraduate Research (Xavier University), 64

Chemical and Engineering News (ACS), 65

Clark, B. R., 17

Clinic Program (Harvey Mudd College), 58–59

College Student Experiences Questionnaire (CSEQ), 38, 45, 46, 54

Communication/writing skills, 34

Community College of Southern Nevada, 65

Community of Scholars (Wofford College), 59

Conference Experience for Undergraduates, 16

Constructivist learning theories, 19–21

Council on Undergraduate Research (CUR), 2, 4, 6, 16, 58, 75

Critical thinking skills, 36

D

Data analysis, 7

Data collection, 7

DEEP (Documenting Effective Educational Practice) project, 29

Department of Energy, 50

E

Environmental effects: construct and elements of environment, 25–26 guiding conceptual framework on, 27*fig* I-E-O (input-environment-outcome) model on role of, 25–27, 79–80 Pascarell'a causal model on, 26–27

Experiential learning, 21–22

F

Faculty: mentor role taken by, 6, 59, 72 percentages of students working with, 48*t*–49*t* undergraduate research/activities outcome for, 40–43 working with students by institutional type/time, 47 *fig*. *See also* Students

Faculty-driven research model, 11

Financial/funding issues, 69–70

Florida State University (FSU), 62–63

Fullerton Foundation, 59

G

General Motors, 69

Global Clinic Program (Harvey Mudd College), 59

Graduate school enrollment, 36–37

Grants for Vertical Integration of Research and Education in Mathematical Sciences, 50

Grinnell College, 42, 59

H

Harold Washington College, 65

Harvey Mudd College (HMC), 58–59

Higher education. *See* Undergraduate education

Historically Black Colleges and Universities Undergraduate Program, 50

Hope College, 60

Howard Hughes Medical Institute, 16, 69

Human resources, 70

Humanities REU (University of South Florida), 63

I

I-E-O (input-environment-outcome) model, 25–27, 79–80

Indiana University, 54

Inquiry-based learning, 22–23

Institutions: liberal arts colleges student engagement efforts, 58–60

multi-institutional student engagement efforts, 65–67

other types of colleges and universities student engagement efforts, 63–65

research universities student engagement efforts, 60–63. *See also* Undergraduate education

Interface (Harvey Mudd College journal), 59

K

Knowledge acquisition: experiential learning approach to, 21–22

inquiry-based learning approach to, 22–23

problem-based learning approach to, 22

L

LEAD Scholars program, 64

Learning. *See* Student learning

Lehrfreiheit (freedom to teach), 14

Lehrnfreiheit (freedom to learn), 14

Liberal arts colleges, 58–60

Louis Stokes Alliance for Minority Participation, 50, 69

M

McNair Program, 39, 40, 51, 69

McNeil, J. A., 8

MAP (Mentored Advanced Project) [Grinnell College], 59

Massachusetts Institute of Technology (MIT), 16, 60–61, 70

Mentors: benefits of, 72

description and role of, 6

Grinnell College's MAP program for, 59

Michigan State University, 66

Minority students, 38–40

Modular Neutron Array [MoNA] project, 51, 65–67

N

National Commission on the Future of Higher Education (2006), 1, 2–3

National Conference for Undergraduate Research (NCUR), 2, 4, 16, 58

National Institutes of Health (NIH), 16

National Science Foundation (NSF), 4, 16, 50, 52, 54, 66, 69, 77

National Superconducting Cyclotron Laboratory (NSCL), 66

National Survey of Student Engagement (NSSE), 28, 45, 47, 54

Northwestern University, 69

About the Authors

Shouping Hu is associate professor of higher education in the Department of Educational Leadership and Policy Studies at Florida State University. His research focuses on postsecondary participation, college student engagement, and higher education finance and policy. He is the author of a 2005 ASHE higher education report, *Beyond Grade Inflation: Grading Problems in Higher Education.*

Kathyrine Scheuch is a doctoral candidate in higher education at Florida State University. Her research interests include undergraduate research activities, minority student issues, and the history of the honors program movement in the United States.

Robert Schwartz is associate professor of higher education in the Department of Educational Leadership and Policy Studies at Florida State University. His research focuses on the history of higher education, women and minorities, and college outcomes.

Joy Gaston Gayles is associate professor of higher education and student affairs in the Department of Adult and Higher Education at North Carolina State University. Her research focuses on the college student experience, campus environments, and college student development.

Shaoqing Li is a senior research analyst in the Office of Institutional Research at Florida A&M University. Her expertise includes information technologies, learning theories, and research methods.

About the ASHE Higher Education Report Series

Since 1983, the ASHE (formerly ASHE-ERIC) Higher Education Report Series has been providing researchers, scholars, and practitioners with timely and substantive information on the critical issues facing higher education. Each monograph presents a definitive analysis of a higher education problem or issue, based on a thorough synthesis of significant literature and institutional experiences. Topics range from planning to diversity and multiculturalism, to performance indicators, to curricular innovations. The mission of the Series is to link the best of higher education research and practice to inform decision making and policy. The reports connect conventional wisdom with research and are designed to help busy individuals keep up with the higher education literature. Authors are scholars and practitioners in the academic community. Each report includes an executive summary, review of the pertinent literature, descriptions of effective educational practices, and a summary of key issues to keep in mind to improve educational policies and practice.

The Series is one of the most peer reviewed in higher education. A National Advisory Board made up of ASHE members reviews proposals. A National Review Board of ASHE scholars and practitioners reviews completed manuscripts. Six monographs are published each year and they are approximately 120 pages in length. The reports are widely disseminated through Jossey-Bass and John Wiley & Sons, and they are available online to subscribing institutions through Wiley InterScience (http://www.interscience.wiley.com).

Call for Proposals

The ASHE Higher Education Report Series is actively looking for proposals. We encourage you to contact one of the editors, Dr. Kelly Ward (kaward@wsu.edu) or Dr. Lisa Wolf-Wendel (lwolf@ku.edu), with your ideas.

Reinventing Undergraduate Education

Recent Titles

ASHE HIGHER EDUCATION REPORT
Order Form
SUBSCRIPTIONS AND SINGLE ISSUES

DISCOUNTED BACK ISSUES:

*Use this form to receive **20% off** all back issues of ASHE Higher Education Report. All single issues priced at **$22.40** (normally $28.00)*

TITLE	ISSUE NO.	ISBN
_____	_____	_____
_____	_____	_____

Call 888-378-2537 *or see mailing instructions below. When calling, mention the promotional code, JB7ND, to receive your discount.*

SUBSCRIPTIONS: *(1 year, 6 issues)*

☐ New Order ☐ Renewal

U.S.	☐ Individual: $165	☐ Institutional: $199
Canada/Mexico	☐ Individual: $165	☐ Institutional: $235
All Others	☐ Individual: $201	☐ Institutional: $310

Call 888-378-2537 *or see mailing and pricing instructions below. Online subscriptions are available at www.interscience.wiley.com.*

Copy or detach page and send to:
John Wiley & Sons, Journals Dept., 5th Floor
989 Market Street, San Francisco, CA 94103-1741

Order Form can also be faxed to: 888-481-2665

	SHIPPING CHARGES:		
Issue/Subscription Amount: $ _____	SURFACE	Domestic	Canadian
Shipping Amount: $ _____	First Item	$5.00	$6.00
(for single issues only—subscription prices include shipping)	Each Add'l Item	$3.00	$1.50
Total Amount: $ _____			

(No sales tax for U.S. subscriptions. Canadian residents, add GST for subscription orders. Individual rate subscriptions must be paid by personal check or credit card. Individual rate subscriptions may not be resold as library copies.)

☐ Payment enclosed (U.S. check or money order only. All payments must be in U.S. dollars.)

☐ VISA ☐ MC ☐ Amex # _____ Exp. Date _____

Card Holder Name _____ Card Issue # _____

Signature_____ Day Phone _____

☐ Bill Me (U.S. institutional orders only. Purchase order required.)

Purchase order # _____
Federal Tax ID13559302   GST 89102 8052

Name_____

Address _____

Phone _____ E-mail _____

JB7ND

ASHE-ERIC HIGHER EDUCATION REPORT IS NOW AVAILABLE ONLINE AT WILEY INTERSCIENCE

What is Wiley InterScience?

Wiley InterScience is the dynamic online content service from John Wiley & Sons delivering the full text of over 300 leading scientific, technical, medical, and professional journals, plus major reference works, the acclaimed Current Protocols laboratory manuals, and even the full text of select Wiley print books online.

What are some special features of Wiley InterScience?

Wiley Interscience Alerts is a service that delivers table of contents via e-mail for any journal available on Wiley InterScience as soon as a new issue is published online.

Early View is Wiley's exclusive service presenting individual articles online as soon as they are ready, even before the release of the compiled print issue. These articles are complete, peer-reviewed, and citable.

CrossRef is the innovative multi-publisher reference linking system enabling readers to move seamlessly from a reference in a journal article to the cited publication, typically located on a different server and published by a different publisher.

How can I access Wiley InterScience?

Visit http://www.interscience.wiley.com.

Guest Users can browse Wiley InterScience for unrestricted access to journal Tables of Contents and Article Abstracts, or use the powerful search engine.

Registered Users are provided with a *Personal Home Page* to store and manage customized alerts, searches, and links to favorite journals and articles. Additionally, Registered Users can view free Online Sample Issues and preview selected material from major reference works.

Licensed Customers are entitled to access full-text journal articles in PDF, with select journals also offering full-text HTML.

How do I become an Authorized User?

Authorized Users are individuals authorized by a paying Customer to have access to the journals in Wiley InterScience. For example, a University that subscribes to Wiley journals is considered to be the Customer.

Faculty, staff and students authorized by the University to have access to those journals in Wiley InterScience are Authorized Users. Users should contact their Library for information on which Wiley journals they have access to in Wiley InterScience.